PURI

A Heavenly Conference

Richard Sibbes

1577–1635

'Of this blest man, let this just praise be given: heaven was in him, before he was in heaven.' So wrote Izaak Walton of Richard Sibbes, lecturer at Holy Trinity, Cambridge, 1610–15; preacher at Gray's Inn, London, from 1616; master of Catherine Hall, Cambridge, from 1626 to his death in 1635. After William Perkins, the 'heavenly' Dr Sibbes was the most significant of the great Puritan preachers of Cambridge, and his writings show the reason why. Strong thoughts, simple sentences, deep knowledge of the Bible and the human heart, and a sure pastoral touch, are here revealed in a sustained concentration on the glory and grace of God in Christ.

Known in his day as 'the sweet dropper' because of the confidence and joy to which his sermons gave rise, Sibbes concentrated on exploring the love, power and patience of Christ, and the riches of the promises of God. He was a pioneer in working out the devotional application of the doctrine of God's covenant grace.

There is no better introduction to the Puritans than the writings of Richard Sibbes, who is, in many ways, a typical Puritan. 'Sibbes never wastes the student's time,' wrote C. H. Spurgeon, 'he scatters pearls and diamonds with both hands.'

Richard Sibbes

A Heavenly Conference

between Christ and Mary after his resurrection,
wherein the intimate familiarity and near
relation between Christ and a believer
is discovered

Jesus saith unto her, Mary. She turned herself, and said to him, Rabboni;
that is to say, Master. And Jesus said to her, Touch me not; for I am not yet
ascended to my Father: but go to my brethren, and say to them, I ascend to
my Father, and your Father; to my God, and your God.— John 20:16, 17.

THE BANNER OF TRUTH TRUST

THE BANNER OF TRUTH TRUST

Head Office
3 Murrayfield Road
Edinburgh, EH12 6EL
UK

North America Office
PO Box 621
Carlisle, PA 17013
USA

banneroftruth.org

First published in 1654
Reprinted from the 1862-64 Nichol edition of
The Works of Richard Sibbes, vol. 6
This edition © The Banner of Truth Trust, 2015
Reprinted 2022

*

ISBN
Print: 978 1 84871 633 9
Epub: 978 1 84871 634 6
Kindle: 978 1 84871 635 3

*

Typeset in 10.5/13.5 Sabon Oldstyle Figures at
The Banner of Truth Trust, Edinburgh

Printed in the USA by
Versa Press Inc.,
East Peoria, IL

Editorial Note:

Footnotes from the Nichol edition of Sibbes' *Works* are attributed to 'G' or 'Ed.' The present publisher has included a few additional footnotes—these are attributed to 'P.' Some spellings have been modernised. Greek words have been transliterated and, along with Latin phrases, explained in footnotes where necessary.

Contents

Foreword by Michael Reeves   vii

To the Reader   xi

A HEAVENLY DISCOURSE BETWEEN CHRIST AND MARY   1

The ministry of angels   2

The apprehension of Christ   4

One word from Christ; one word from Mary   8

Application   11

Communion with Christ   19

     Beware of apathy   20

     Beware of formality   23

A particular interest in Christ   24

Christ's prohibition   26

     Outward things   27

Christ's commission   32

Christ our brother   35

     The comfort of being Christ's brethren   43

     The dignity of Christ's brethren   47

     Christ's timing   49

     Christ's love constant and invincible   51

Christ's love to his cast down brethren 54

The matter of Christ's commission 62

Christ's ascension and ours 63

The purpose of Christ's ascension 68

Christ pleading our cause 73

The comfort of an ascended Christ 75

Christ's Father and ours 80

The comfort of having God as our Father 92

God's love in Christ 94

Be indulgent in preaching the truth 98

Knowing true brethren 101

The priority of Christ's relation to the Father 105

Christ's God and ours 111

The comfort in God being our God 115

Application 120

God sovereign in our hearts 120

God the ground of our obedience 123

God all-sufficient for us 142

Assurance of salvation 152

Foreword

O N the first Easter morning, Mary Magdalene had the first encounter with the risen Christ. They exchanged only a few words, but Richard Sibbes (1577–1635) saw in that meeting the gospel in a nutshell. For in that moment in the garden he saw how the risen Saviour deals with a believer.

A Heavenly Conference is Sibbes' exposition of both that moment and the broader truth it captures: our union with Christ. His intent was that we should enjoy the comfort that comes from knowing God as our God and Father, and knowing Christ as our brother. For, when we are united to Christ we can know we share the secure standing of our firstborn brother before God our Father. As Sibbes argues, God

> can as soon cease to love his Son, as cease to love us. For with the same love he loveth all Christ mystical, head and members. There is not the least finger of Christ, the least despised member of Christ, but God looketh on him with that sweet eternal tenderness with which he looketh upon his Son, preserving the prerogative of the head. Oh, this is a sweet comfort, that now all the excellent privileges of a Christian are set on Christ and

then on us and therefore we should not lose them, for Christ will lose nothing.

A key moment in that garden-meeting is when Jesus speaks of returning 'to my Father and your Father, to my God and your God' (John 20:17). This, Sibbes believed,

> is the most fundamental comfort that we have. For from this, that God is our God, cometh all that we have that is good in nature and grace. Whatsoever is comfortable cometh from this spring, that God in Christ is our God, our reconciled God.

Without such assurance, we simply cannot live Christian lives as God would have us. God would have us thankful, cheerful, rejoicing and strong in faith: but we will be none of these things unless we are sure that God and Christ are ours for good. Here, then, are pastorally vital truths that Sibbes seeks to work into us.

But there is something about Sibbes – both here and in all his works – that goes beyond the content. Writers in his day would have called it a 'tincture': an atmosphere or tone about the man. For there is more to Sibbes than theological correctness or even pastoral wisdom: he exudes an irresistible delight in Christ.

That helps to explain a shrewd observation made by the authors of the original preface to this work: Sibbes, they suggest, consciously sought to undo the sort of dead orthodoxy where doctrines get treated as mere balls in a game of theological ping-pong. They called it 'that itch of questions and disputings, like a noxious humour', and wrote of Sibbes remedying it by captivating people 'with the inward beauty and glory of Christ'. That, surely, is as necessary today as ever: Christians today need not only the truth and comfort Sibbes offers here; they need his heartfelt delight so that they live for no other end than the very glory of God.

MICHAEL REEVES
Oxford
June 2015

To the Reader

The scope and business of this epistle is not so much to commend the workman—whose name is a sweet savour in the church—as to give thee a short summary-view of the generals handled in this treatise. Though much might be said of this eminent saint, if either detraction had fastened her venomous nails in his precious name, or the testimony of the subscribers of this epistle might give the book a freer admission into thy hands. This only we shall crave leave to mind the reader of, that this bright star, who sometimes with his light refreshed the souls of God's people while he shone in the horizon of our church, set, as we may say, between the evening of many shadows and the morning of a bright hoped-for Reformation; which, though it be for the present overcast, yet being so agreeable to the mind of Jesus Christ, and ushered in with the groans and prayers of so many of his saints, we doubt not but will in God's own time break forth gloriously, to the dissipating of those clouds and fogs which at the present do eclipse and darken it.

Now, as it is the wisdom of God, in bringing about his own designs, to raise up fit and suitable instruments for the work of every generation, so it is also the gracious dispensation of God to put seasonable words into the mouths of those his servants, who by faith do fix their eyes on him for the guidance of his blessed Spirit; as every judicious reader may observe in the works of this reverend divine, who foreseeing, as it were, what a degeneracy of spirit professors[1] in his time were falling apace into, that itch of questions and disputings, like a noxious humour, beginning then to break forth among professors,[2] like a skilful physician, applied himself to preserve the vitals and essentials of religion, that the souls of his hearers, being captivated with the inward beauty and glory of Christ, and being led into an experimental knowledge of heavenly truths, their spirits might not evaporate and discharge themselves in endless, gainless, soul-unedifying, and conscience-perplexing questions. For as it is in nature, a man that hath tasted the sweetness of honey will not easily be persuaded that honey is bitter, but he that hath only taken it up upon credit may soon be baffled out of it, because no act can go higher than its principles; and so it is in religion. For those good souls that have embraced the truths of Jesus Christ upon a supernatural principle, and experimented not only the truth, but the goodness of them in their own souls, they are the clinched Christians, the good hold-fast men, as Mr Fox styles some Christians in his days; they are the even and steady walkers. Whereas those that have only a 'form of godliness' (2 Tim. 3:5), a slight tincture – who have only out of novelty and curiosity, or pride and ambition, or other self ends, professed religion – will prove giddy and unconstant, 'like clouds carried about with every blast'

[1] That is, 'professing Christians'. — P.
[2] In margin here, *Pruritus disputandi scabies ecclesiae* [The itch of disputation is the scab or tetter of the church]. — Sir H. Wotton. — G.

(Eph. 4:14), and while they promise themselves liberty, be a prey to the net of every fancy and opinion.

To the sound and practical Christian that is not squeesy-stomached,[1] will the truths in this treatise be grateful. Supposing therefore and desiring, if thou art not, thou mayest be such a one, here is offered to thy consideration a divine and heavenly discourse betwixt Christ and Mary, between a soul-burdened sinner and a burden-removing Saviour.

That thou mayest here see how diligent Mary is to seek, how ready Christ is to be found. Mary hath her heart brimful of sorrow; Christ comes, as it were, 'leaping over the mountains' (Song of Sol. 2:8), with comfort and bowels[2] of compassion. Mary was in a strong pang of affection, nay, her affections were wound so high that her expressions seem broken; and her actions might seem to savour of irregularity, were it not that the excellency of the object did warrant the height of her affection, and the compassion of Christ was large enough, not only to interpret for the best, but also to pardon and cover all her infirmities. The woman was better at her affections than expressions. 'They have taken away my Lord.' She speaks at random, names nobody, whether Jews, or disciples, or soldiers. But see the strength of her faith. She is not ashamed to call him 'Lord', even in the lowest state of humiliation. Though Christ be reproached, persecuted, despised, rejected, dead, buried, yet he shall be Mary's Lord. Again, 'I know not where

---

[1] That is, 'queezy', 'squeamish', = rising on the stomach.—G.
[2] Used in the sense of the heart, denoting pity and tenderness (the emotions being supposed to be seated in the bowels).—P.

they have laid him.' She dreams of a bodily asportation[1] and resting of Christ somewhere, and speaks with indignation, as if she looked upon it as an indignity or incivility, nay, of cruelty—*Saevitum est in cadavera, saevitum est in ossa, saevitum est in cineres*[2] (Cyprian)—of the Roman emperors' cruelty, to remove a dead body. What was done to Christ, Mary takes it as done to her; and, good heart, she thinks she hath so much right to him, that he should not be stirred without her knowledge. And 'I know not where', *etc.*

Now while Mary is seeking Christ – who is never far absent from a seeking soul – he stands at her back. Christ is nearer to us many times than we think of. Sometimes a poor soul wants the sight of comfort more than matter of comfort, and is, like Hagar, weeping for water when the well is hard by. Seeking of Christ is the soul's duty; but Christ manifesting himself is the soul's comfort. Mary turned herself, and she saw Jesus. Gerson saith, the angels rose up at the presence of Christ, which Mary seeing, made her turn about.[3] But omitting that conjecture, the original word στρεφεσθαι [*strephesthai*] is sometimes used for a turning of the face, but most frequently for a turning of the whole body. But to put it out of doubt here, it is said

---

[1] That is, 'a carrying away'. Cf. Richardson, *sub voce*.—G.

[2] Latin: 'An act of cruelty towards corpses, towards bones and towards ashes.' This Father has many eloquent passages on the reverence due to the 'body' of the believer, as formerly a 'temple' of the Holy Ghost; and the present is a reminiscence of one of them.—P.

[3] In margin here, '*Ideo conversa est quia angeli assurrexerunt presentiae Christi.*'—Gerson. Latin: 'She turned because the angels rose at the presence of Christ.'—P.

exegetically, ἐστραφη εἰς τὰ ὀπίσω [*estraphe eis ta opiso*], 'she turned herself back'—the same phrase the Septuagint uses of Lot's wife looking back.[1] Many times Christ hath his face towards us, when we have our backs upon him; and therefore if thou wouldst find Christ, turn thyself to him.

Again, here thou mayest see the true Joseph. He knows Mary when she knows not him, but takes him for the gardener. Christ is always beforehand with us in his grace. He loves us before we love him, and calls us before we call him. Mary travails with desires to find Christ, and Christ is full of yearnings towards her. Like Joseph, he could restrain no longer, and because the general manifestations of Christ wrought little, he calls her by her name, 'Mary'; and she being a sheep of Christ, 'knows his voice', and answers him with a title of dignity, *Rabboni;* that is to say, 'My Master.'

We may see here that discoveries of grace are not fruitless. They stir up believers' reverence and obedience. 'Let us sin because grace abounds', is the devil's application of Christ's doctrine (Rom. 6:1).

These and several other particulars are with much brevity, spirituality, and perspicuity handled in this treatise, and with that liveliness that they show they come from one whose own heart savoured what he taught to others. The largest part of this book is spent upon that sweet doctrine, viz., *a believer's interest in God as a Father, and the comforts that flow from that sweet relation.* The

---

[1] Gen. 19:26 in the LXX is as follows: Καὶ ἐπέβλεψεν ἡ γυνὴ αὐτοῦ εἰς τὰ ὀπίσω [*Kai epeblepsen he gune autou eis ta opiso*] i.e., *se domum versa praeter virum suum qui subsequebatur ipsam.*—Junius *in anal, in Gen.*—G. Latin: 'turning towards her home beyond her husband who was following her.'—P.

foundation of our relation to God is here handled, and how God is first a Father to Christ, and in him to us. What can be more comfortable in this earthly, interest-shaking, disjointing, confounding age, than to clear up our soul's interest in God? *Tolle meum, et tolle deum*, as he said.[1] It were better for me there were no God, than that he should not be my God. This will be thy comfort, that when thou canst not say, 'My state, my liberty, my house, my land, my friend, my trade', thou mayest be able to say, 'My Father, my God'. If therefore thou savourest the things of God, this subject will be acceptable and grateful to thee; and if this treatise may be any ways instrumental for putting thee upon study how to get it, or upon practice how to improve it, or in case thy soul sits in darkness, how to endear and clear thy interest, the publishers shall have much of their aim, and thou wilt have no cause to repent thy cost in buying, or thy pains in reading. We shall add no more than this. Blessed is that man or woman that hath an interest in him who is the Father of Jesus Christ by eternal generation, and of all believers in Christ by adoption and regeneration; in which inheritance and portion, that thou mayest have a share, shall be the prayer of

> Thy soul's and thy faith's servants in the work of the ministry for Jesus' sake,

Simon Ash

James Nalton

Joseph Church

---

[1] Latin: 'Take away that word *my*, and take away that word *God*.' Qu. Bernard? — G.

A Heavenly Discourse between Christ and Mary, after His Resurrection

Jesus saith unto her, Mary. She turned herself, and said to him, Rabboni; that is to say, Master. And Jesus said to her, Touch me not; for I am not yet ascended to my Father: but go to my brethren, and say to them, I ascend to my Father, and your Father; to my God, and your God. — John 20:16, 17.

The same love of Christ that drew him from heaven to the womb of the virgin, from the womb of the virgin to the cross, and from the cross to the grave, the same love of Christ moved him to discover himself after he was risen from the grave to them that he knew did entirely and wonderfully love him. And therefore, before he would ascend to heaven, he did vouchsafe many apparitions[1] and discoveries of himself, partly to instruct them in the certainty of his resurrection, and partly, but especially, to comfort them: those that he knew did love him.

His first apparition of all was made to Mary, the woman out of whom he had cast seven devils (Luke 8:2). She was much beholding to him, and therefore

[1] That is, 'appearances'. — G.

loved much (Luke 7:47). No sex may discourage any sinner from Christ. She expresseth her love of Christ by her desire of finding him, by her seeking and weeping, notwithstanding all impediments, before she found him.

The ministry of angels

As she wept, she stooped down and looked into the sepulchre, and there saw two angels in white: a colour of glory, purity, and joy, because it was a time of joy. They were one at the head, and the other at the feet. As in the law, when the mercy-seat was made, two cherubims were also framed, and placed one at the one end, and the other at the other end thereof, with their faces looking one towards another (Exod. 25:20). And when Christ was risen, there were two angels, one at the head, another at the feet, to show that peace was to be expected in the true propitiatory, Jesus Christ.

One at the head, the other at the feet of the body of Jesus. And they sat there. It was a time of peace. Peace was made between heaven and earth, God and man; and here is a posture of peace, 'They sat quietly.' In Christ, angels and we are at one; God, and we, and all. There is a recapitulation and gathering of all things in heaven and earth (Col. 1:20).

The angels, they attended on Christ in all the passages of his life and death till they brought him to heaven.[1]

---

[1] In margin here, 'Ministry of angels towards Christ. Luke 2:9, 10; Luke 22:43; John 12:29; Acts 1:10; Heb. 1:14; Psa. 34:7; Luke 16:22; Matt. 24:31.' — G.

They brought news of his birth, comforted him in his agony; they were at his resurrection, and you see here they attend. At his ascension they accompany him. And as they did to the Head, so they will to the members. In our infancy, they take charge of our tender years; in our dangers, they pitch their tents about us; in our deaths, they carry our souls to Abraham's bosom, a place of happiness. At our resurrection, their office is to gather our bodies together. That service and attendance they afforded the Head they afford to the members; to mystical Christ as well as natural. Therefore let us comfort ourselves in the service they did to Christ.

Now, besides the apparition of the angels, here is the speech of the angels: 'Woman, why weepest thou?' They knew she had no cause of weeping, for Christ whom she sought was risen again.

She answereth, 'Because they have taken away my Lord, and I know not where they have laid him.' If it had been as she supposed, there had been cause enough of her weeping, if her Lord had been taken away; for when the Lord is taken away, what remaineth that is comfortable? And if the Lord be not taken away, it matters not what is taken away. For he is all in all. Carnal people, so they have their wealth, and friends, and comforts in the world, they care not what is taken away. But she is of another mind. 'They have taken away my Lord', and what comfort can I have if my Lord be taken away?

But it was but the speech of an opinion; she did but think it. And there were two things might lead her, truth and probability, which is the foundation of opinion. *Probability:* he is not here, therefore he is taken away. *Truth:* Christ promised he would rise again, therefore he would take away himself. There was certain truth to ground faith, and weak probability to ground opinion. Yet such is the nature of weak persons in distress. If there be probability and certain truth, yet they will be sure to cleave to their probabilities. Oh, theirs be great sin! Ay, but there is greater mercy for faith to lay hold upon. So the presumptuous sinner saith, 'God is merciful.' Ay, but God hath excluded thee from heaven; thou art an adulterer, a swearer, a filthy person; thy opinion is grounded scarce upon probability. 'God is merciful', but not to such sinners as live in sins against reconciliation as thou dost (1 Cor. 6:9). Therefore, when one hath but probability to ground opinion, and the other certain truth to ground faith, be so wise for our souls as to take the best and leave the other. If she had remembered his promise to raise himself out of the grave, she needed not to have doubted.

'They have taken away my Lord, and I know not where they have laid him.' '*They* have taken away.' She instanceth none. And when she had thus said, she turneth her back, and saw Jesus standing, and knew not that it was Jesus. The angels hold their peace when Christ speaks, and it is their place so to do.

The apprehension of Christ
But she knew not that it was Jesus in respect of her

passion.[1] Her senses were held partly by the power of God, and partly by a kind of passion that was a cloud between her and Jesus, that she knew him not at that time.

What doth Jesus say to her?

'Woman, why weepest thou? whom seekest thou?' The first words that ever Christ spake after his resurrection to them he appeared to, is, 'Woman, why weepest thou?' It is a good question after Christ's resurrection. What cause of weeping when Christ is risen? Our sins are forgiven, because he, our head and surety, hath suffered death for us; and if Christ be risen again, why weep we? If we be broken-hearted, humbled sinners, that have interest in his death and resurrection, we have no cause to grieve. It is therefore a good question to them that believe, 'Why weepest thou? whom seekest thou?' They were questions, not for satisfaction to him – he knew it well enough – but to draw out her mind, and to draw out by confession what God had hid in her heart, that he might comfort her afterwards.

'But she, supposing him to be the gardener, said, Sir, if thou hast borne him hence, tell me', *etc*.

She had a misconceit of Christ, as if he had been the gardener. Beloved, so it is with a sinner, especially in times of desolation of spirit and disconsolate condition. They present Christ to themselves as an enemy. She

---

[1] strong feeling of sorrow or sorrowful agitation of mind. – P.

in passion thinks Christ the gardener. Do not many, when they be melancholy of body and troubled in mind, conceive of Christ as an austere judge, that will undoubtedly damn such wretches as they are, who present Christ to themselves in that fashion, that the Scripture doth not? Doth not he bid all that be weary and heavy laden come to him? (Matt. 11:28). And yet they, out of passion, will present Christ to be an austere judge, that will take them at their disadvantage, observe all their ways, and will surely damn them.

It is a great violence that passion and opinion offers to truth, and to saving truth, and the hardest matter in the world for a distressed conscience to apprehend God aright, and to apprehend Christ aright. Secure persons apprehend God under a false notion. They apprehend God as a God all of mercy, and Christ as if he were not a judge of the world; as if he observed them not, nor their sinful courses; and therefore they care not whether they serve him or no (Acts 17:31). And Satan presenteth Christ all of mercy, and Satan and their hearts meeting together, the mistake is dangerous. It is a great art of faith, and an excellent skill, to apprehend Christ suitable to our condition that we are in. When we be in any sin, then think him a judge; then think of Moses rather than of Christ; then think of Christ as one that will judge both quick and dead for their hard and wicked actions. But when we be humble and broken-hearted, and touched with sense of sin, present him as a sweet Saviour, inviting and alluring all to come to him: 'Come to me, all ye', *etc.*, (Matt. 11:28); present him as a gentle shepherd; present him in all the sweet relations he names himself by in the Scriptures, lest otherwise we do Christ dishonour, and ourselves wrong (Isa. 40:11).

'If thou hast borne him hence, tell me where thou hast laid him, and I will take him away.'

She was a likely woman indeed to take Christ away; for a weak woman to take a heavy body away! But love thinks nothing impossible. Faith and love agree in this, nothing is impossible. 'Love is strong as death' (Song of Sol. 8:6). Neither love nor faith care for difficulties; they arm the soul to break through all.

'Tell me where thou hast laid him, and I will take him away.'

One would think the dead body might have frighted the woman, and the heavy body might have been above her strength. But she was in such an ecstasy of love and desire, and grief for want of desire, that she considered not well what she said.

They be words of passion; and, indeed, if you observe the story of Mary Magdalene, she was a woman of extremity in all conditions. Like Jonah, when he grieves, he grieves exceedingly; when he rejoices, his joy is wound to the highest pitch. So she was full of love when she loved, and full of grief when she grieved, and full of joy when she joyed. She had large affections. All were in the highest measure, and strained to the highest pin in her; and that made her say, 'If thou hast', *etc.*

One word from Christ; one word from Mary

Jesus could not endure [to keep] her longer in this perplexed condition. He was too merciful; and therefore saith, 'Mary'. She turned to him, and saith, 'Rabboni', which is to say, Master.

And Jesus said to her, 'Mary'.

The words are a sweet and loving intercourse between Christ and Mary. In a seasonable time, when she was in all her perplexity and depth of sorrow for loss of her Lord, Christ seasonably at length, as not being able to hold any longer, but must needs discover himself, saith to her, 'Mary'.

You see, first of all, Christ beginneth, and saith, 'Mary'; she answereth, in the second place, and saith, 'Rabboni'; and till Christ begins, no voice in the world can do any good. The angels they spake to her, but till Christ spake nothing could comfort her. Christ began, and till Christ began nothing would comfort Mary. Christ began himself, and used but one word. It is a word, and but one word. Nothing will comfort but the word of Christ. The word that comforted her when he spake, and it was but one word, and yet enough, there was such fulness of spirit and comfort in that one word. And she answereth with one word again.

You may ask why they spake but one word. Beloved, he was full of affection, and she was full of affection also, too full to express themselves in many words. As it is in grief, grief sometimes may be so great that scarce any words are able to express it: *ingentes dolores stupent*;[1] and if any words, then broken words, which show fulness of affection rather than any distinct sense. Christ was so full, and she so full, that a word discovers. And indeed there was so much sense, and so much love, so much contained in these little words 'Mary' and 'Rabboni', that it is impossible to express them shorter; and her passion would not stay any longer discourse. It was by words, and by one word, 'Mary'. It was by a word which showeth he took notice of her. Christ knows the names of the stars; he knows everything by name. He knows everything of a man, to the very hair. He knows their parts, and their very excrements[2] of their parts. He knew her, and acknowledged her too: 'Mary'.

1. It is a word of knowledge, and familiar acquaintance, and acknowledgment.

2. It is a word of compassion; because he had held her long, and now could not longer. He pitieth the state she was in. He saw her ready to sink for grief and melt for sorrow, and therefore he said, 'Mary'.

3. As it is a word of compassion, so it is a word full of exceeding love.

4. And it is a word of peculiar appropriation, 'Mary', whom I have so much respected heretofore. And a word of satisfaction on his part, out of his pity, and out of his love, and former familiarity and acquaintance. 'Mary', I am the man that thou seekest;

---

[1] Latin: 'great griefs stupefy.' —P.

[2] *i.e.*, outgrowths, *e.g.*, the hairs that grow out of one's head. —P.

I know what all thy seekings tend to. Thou wantest him whom thou lovest; thou wantest me; I am he whom thou seekest.

She answered him again, 'Rabboni', which is interpreted, Master. She returned him an answer again; she spake to him. He first began, then she follows. She found the virtue of his speech in her heart. There was an influence of it to her heart; and his love witnessing to her heart, raised her love to him again. So it was an answer of Christ's speech, and from the same affection: an answer of love, and an answer of exceeding large affection and satisfaction to her soul. O my 'Rabboni', the soul of my soul, the life of my life, my joy, my rock, my all that can be dear to me. 'Rabboni', I have enough. As he desired to give her satisfaction, so she takes satisfaction in the word. And yet it was not full satisfaction; for after she clasps about him, and would not let him go. It was an affection that stirred up much desire more and more to have communion with him, so that he was fain to check her afterward: 'Touch me not, for I am not yet ascended to my Father.' She had not enough; as indeed a believing, affectionate soul hath never enough till it be in heaven.

And thus you see the sweet intercourse upon the apparition and first discovery of Christ to Mary. He spake to her, and she answered him again with the same affection. And it is a word of dependence, as it is fit, 'Rabboni, my Master'. It is not only a word of honour, not any superior, but a superior in way of teaching.

There was submission of conscience to the 'Rabboni', as the 'Rabboni', labouring to sit in the consciences of people. It is a Syriac word, which signifieth in the original, 'multiplication of knowledge' in him that speaketh, and that laboureth to breed much knowledge in him that is spoken to; and therefore it is a word of great respect and dependence.[1]

She might well call him 'Rabboni', for he was 'Master of masters', 'Rabboni of rabbonis', the angel of the covenant, the great doctor of the church, the great 'Gamaliel', at whose feet all must sit and be taught. So you see what sense and affections are in these little words. The fulness of heart that was in this couple cannot be expressed, were it possible to say all that could be said.

Application
And therefore we leave the hypothesis, and come to make application of it to ourselves.

Obs. 1. First, *We may learn here, that till Christ himself discovers himself, no teaching will serve the turn.* No. The teaching of angels will not serve the turn, till Christ himself by his Holy Spirit discovers himself. When Christ doth it, it is done. And therefore it should teach us so to attend upon the ministry as to look up to the great doctor that hath his chair in heaven, and

[1] By Syriac, Sibbes means Hebrew, a common use of the term by him and his contemporaries. —G.

teacheth the heart.[1] If he teach, it is no matter how dull the scholar is. He is able to make any scholar, if he instruct. I will not enlarge the point, because there be particular places wherein they will be enlarged.

Obs. 2. The second thing I will observe is this, *that Christ, when he teacheth, he doth it by words, not by crucifixes, not by sights.* We lost our salvation and all our happiness by the ear, and we must come to it by the ear again. Adam, by hearkening to Eve, and Eve to the serpent, lost all; and we must recover salvation therefore by the ear. As we have heard, so we shall see. We must first hear, and then see. Life cometh in at the ear as well as death. Faith, you know, is the quickening of a Christian, the spiritual life of a Christian. Now, faith comes by hearing; and therefore I beseech you in the bowels of Christ, set aside prejudice, and meekly attend God's ordinances. Do not consider who we are; we are but poor ministers, frail men as yourselves. But consider the Lord, that is pleased to convey life, and salvation, and grace, and whatsoever is fit to bring to heaven, this way. Therefore they that despise this way, set light by salvation; as the apostle saith (Acts 13:46), 'They judge themselves unworthy of the kingdom of heaven.' They can read at home, but is that the way God hath sanctified? Did not the manna stink when

[1] In margin here, '*Cathedram habet in cælis qui corda docet*,'—G. Latin: 'He has his pulpit in heaven who teaches the heart.'—P.

gathered on the Sabbath day? There is a curse upon all private industry and devotion when it is with neglect of public ordinances. She could have no comfort till Christ spake. Nay, the very sight of Christ could not comfort her. Let this, I pray you, be enough, that I may not enlarge the point any further. This is the way for comfort. We must hear him in his ministers here, if we will hear him comfortably speaking to us hereafter, 'Come, ye blessed of my Father', *etc.* (Matt. 25:34).

Obs. 3. It was but one word, 'Mary'; and is there so much force in one word? Yea, when it is uttered by Christ. One word coming from Christ, and set on the heart by the Spirit of Christ, hath a mighty efficacy. The word hath an efficacy in creating all things, *fiat*, *fuit*. Let it be done: it was done; 'Let there be light: there was light.' So let there be light in the understanding, and there it shall be presently. So in all Christ's cures, he said the word, and it was done. So in all spiritual cures, let him say the word, it is done. Nay, a very look of Christ, if the Spirit go along with it, is able to convert the soul. *Respexit Christus, flevit Petrus amarè:* Christ looked on Peter, he wept bitterly. What will his word do, when his look will do so much? It was but a word, and but one word: 'Say but the word', saith he in the gospel, 'and my servant shall be healed' (Matt. 8:8). This should make us desire that Christ would speak though but few words to the soul; that he would clothe the words of men mightily with his word and with his

Spirit; and then they will be mighty in operation and works. One word, but it was a pregnant word. It was full of affection. She knew it well enough: 'Mary'. What! to call her so familiarly, so sweetly, by her accustomed name? It wrought on her bowels[1] presently.

Obs. 4. But to go on. You see here again, *that Christ must begin to us before we can answer him.* He began to 'Mary', and then she said 'Rabboni'. All the passages of salvation are done by way of covenant, by way of commerce and intercourse between God and man, but God begins first. In election, indeed, we choose him; but he chooseth us first. And he knoweth who are his, and we know him; but he knows us first. And in calling, we answer, Ay; but he calleth first, and we do but echo to his call. In justification, forgiveness of sins, we accept of justification, and submit to the righteousness of Christ, and God's purpose of saving man that way; but he giveth faith first, for faith is the gift of God. We glorify him here on earth, but it is from a result of God's glorifying us in heaven. Some earnests[2] we have, but they are of God's giving. All we do is but reflection of his love first, or his knowledge first.

The Christian soul saith, 'Thou art my God'; ay, but he saith first, 'I am thy salvation' (Psa. 35:3). As Augustine saith, *Non frustra dicit anima, Deus salus tua:*[3]

---

[1] on her heart, or emotions.—P.

[2] Earnests: payments given in token of an agreement or covenant.—P.

[3] Latin: 'The soul is not wasting its time when it says, "God,

when God saith, 'I am thy salvation', it is easy for the soul to say, 'Thou art my God'. And this may teach us in our devotions, when we are to deal with God, when we are to bring to him any request, to desire him first to reveal himself to us, desire Christ to reveal himself by his Spirit to us. It is an error in the case of men's devotions. They think to bring something of their own strength, and to break in, as it were, upon God, without his discovery first. But Paul saith (Gal. 4:9), 'We know God, or rather, are known of him.' We must desire that he would make known his heart to us first, and then we shall know him again; that he would speak to us by his Spirit, and then we shall answer to him again. That he would say to our souls, he 'is our salvation'; and then we may lay claim to him, 'he is our God'. Desire the 'Spirit of revelation', to reveal his bowels and love to us in Christ by his Holy Spirit; for certainly, in every return of ours to Christ, God begins to us, all in all, though not sensibly. But we ought to pray, every day more and more, for a sensible[1] revelation, that God would reveal his love to us in Christ. And we cannot but answer. If Christ saith, 'Mary', Mary cannot but answer, 'Rabboni'.

Obj. But you will say then, It is not our fault, but Christ's fault, if he must begin. If God begins, we shall answer.

---

you are my salvation.'" —P.

[1] *i.e.*, a revelation perceived or felt by the senses. —P.

Ans. I answer briefly, that God doth always begin to us, and is beforehand with us in all dealings with ourselves. He giveth us many motions, and never withdraweth himself from us, but when he is despised and slighted first; therefore, let us take heed that we labour to answer Christ's call when he doth call. If we slight it, then in a judicious[1] course he ceaseth to speak further to us, if we slight his beginnings of revelations. There be many degrees and passages to faith and assurance. If we do not observe the beginning, how God begins to reveal himself to us by little and little, speaking to us by his Spirit in our hearts when he begins, then in a spiritual judgment sometimes he leaves us to ourselves. And therefore let us regard all the motions of the Spirit, and all the speeches of the Spirit of Christ, for he begins by little and little, else our consciences will say afterward, we are not saved, because we would not be saved. We would not yield to all the passages of salvation; but when he was beforehand with us, and offered many sweet motions, yet we loved our sins better than our souls, and so repelled all. Therefore, I beseech you, do not refuse the sweet messages from heaven, the gracious and sweet motions of the Spirit of Christ.[2] Make much of them. God hath begun to you, be sure to answer. Learn it of Mary. When Christ began, she set not her heart and infidelity against it,

[1] Qu. 'judicial'?—G.

[2] In margin here, '*Alloquenti Christo fideles respondent.*'—G. Latin: 'When Christ speaks the believers respond.'—P.

but she opened her heart, and said, 'Rabboni'; learn, therefore, the duty of spiritual obedience. When God speaks, 'Speak, Lord, for thy servant heareth' (1 Sam. 3:10). Do not shut your ears to the motions of God's blessed Spirit; do not harden your hearts against his voice, but open your hearts as she did: 'Rabboni'.

Our Saviour Christ here saith, 'Mary'; but when? After he had concealed himself from her a long time. It is not presently 'Mary', nor 'Rabboni'. He had concealed himself a great while. Christ doth not usually open himself fully at first, though at first he doth in some degree; but he observeth degrees, as in the church in general. You see how that he discovers himself in his gracious promises by little and little; darkly at first, and at last the Sun of righteousness ariseth clearly. So the day-star ariseth in our hearts by degrees. It is a great while before Mary heareth the satisfying speech of Christ, 'Mary.'

Quest. But why doth Christ thus conceal himself in regard of his fuller manifestation?

It is partly to try and exercise our faith and other graces; and therefore God doth seem to withdraw himself in the sense of his love.

1. *To see whether we can live by faith,* or whether we be altogether addicted to sense, as the world is, who live altogether by sense, and not by faith.

2. *He would have our patience tried to the utmost.* He would have 'patience have its perfect work' (James 1:4).

She had much patience to endure all this. But her patience had not a perfect work till Christ spake.

3. *Christ will stir up and quicken zeal and fervency in his children;* and therefore he seemed to deny the woman of Canaan (Matt. 15:21, *seq.*, and Mark 7:27, 28); first, he giveth no answer but an harsh answer, 'A dog'. And she works upon it: 'Though I am a dog, yet dogs have crumbs.' All which denial was only to stir up zeal and earnestness. And therefore though Christ doth not manifest himself to us at first, yet it is to stir up zeal and affection to seek after him more earnestly. A notable passage there is of this (Song of Sol. 3:1-4). The soul sought Christ, and sought long, and sought in the use of all means; but at length she waited, and in waiting she found him.

4. *Christ doth this to set a better price upon his presence when he comes;* to make his presence highly valued when he doth discover himself. *Desiderata diu magis placent:* things long desired please more sweetly. And things, when wanted, are ingratiated to us, as warmth after cold, and meat after hunger; and so in every particular of this life. And therefore God, to set a greater price on his presence, and that he would be held more strongly when he doth reveal himself, he defers a long time. That is one reason why he did defer revealing himself to Mary, that she might have the more sweet contentment in him when he did reveal himself, as indeed she had. Long deferring of a thing doth but enlarge the soul. Want enlargeth the desire and capacity

of the soul, so doth love. Now, when we want that we love, that emptieth the soul marvellously much; it mortifieth affection. When God keeps off a long time, and we see it is God only must do it, then the affection is taken off from earthly things, and the heart enlarged to God by love, and the want of the thing we love. And therefore we set a price on the thing, so that we are wonderfully pleasing to God. It is very beneficial to ourselves. What lost Mary by it? So shall we lose nothing. We have it at last more abundantly. We have it as a mighty favour. Mary taketh this as a new blessing altogether. When things are kept long from us, and God only must discover, when the heart is kept from second causes, the heart is enlarged. Certainly this comes from God, and God should have all the glory of it. God is wise; and therefore makes us to stay a long time for that we do desire.

Communion with Christ

We all of us are in Mary's case in a spiritual sense. Sometimes or other we miss Christ, I mean the sweet sense of Christ. Lay this down for a rule, that Christians ought to walk in sweet communion with God and Christ, and that it ought to be the life of a Christian to maintain the communion that Christ hath vouchsafed between us and himself. Then, certainly, we lose Christ wonderfully; and not against our minds, but willingly, by our own slighting of him, and by our own under-valuing of him, or by our negligence or presumption.

Christ, though he be low, yet he is great, and he will have us to know his greatness. There must be communion with due respect. One way or other we deprive ourselves of the sense and sweetness of communion with Christ. What must we do, then? We must do as the woman did: turn over every stone; use all kind of means; leave not one till we find him; and when all means are used, wait still. Persevere in waiting, as Peter speaks. Believers, wait; hold out in waiting, for Christ in his time will come. He cannot hold long. As Joseph did suppress his love and affection for politic ends a great while (Gen. 45:3), but his pity towards his brethren was such that his bowels would not suffer him to conceal himself longer; his passion was above his policy: 'I am Joseph.' And so let us in the use of all things seek Christ and the sweet sense of his love, which is better than life itself. And, indeed, what is all without Christ? Christ is so full of compassion, he will not long suffer us to be prolonged, but will at length satisfy the hungry soul (Psa. 63:5). How many promises have we to this end!

Beware of apathy
Take heed of such a temper of soul, as cares not whether we find Christ or no. Oh take heed of that! If we will seek him, seek him as Mary. She sought him early in the morning; she brake her sleep and sought him with tears. If anything be to be sought with tears, it is Christ and communion with him. She sought him instantly and constantly. She sought him so, that no

impediment could hinder her, she was so full of grief and love.[1] She sought him with her whole heart, she waited in seeking. That is the way to find Christ. Seek him early, in our younger times, in the morning of our years. Oh that we could seek Christ as we seek our pleasures. We should find more pleasure in Christ than in all the pleasures of the world, if we could persuade our base hearts so much. Seek him above all other things. Awake with this resolution in our hearts, to find Christ, never to be quiet till we may say with some comfort, 'I am Christ's, and Christ is mine.' When we have him, we have all. Seek him with tears, at length we are sure to find him. He hath bound himself, that if we knock he will open; and if we seek we shall find: if we seek wisdom early with our whole hearts, entirely, sincerely. Seek Christ for Christ, and then we shall be sure to find him, as she did. Thus seek him in the word and sacraments, wherein he discovers himself familiarly. Seek him in the temple – 'Christ was found in the temple' (Luke 2:46) – and then we shall be sure to find him both here and hereafter. Specially we shall find him in our hearts. You see how familiarly he comes to us in the word, speaks to us by a man like ourselves. And how familiarly by the sacrament, by common bread and common wine, sanctified to do great matters above nature, to strengthen faith. He cometh to us through our faces, into our souls in

[1] In margin here, 'Matt. 28:1; Mark 16:9; Luke 24:1; John 20:1.' – G.

the sacrament. He cometh to us, through our ears in hearing the word, through our sight in seeing the bread broken. He comes by familiar things, and by a familiar manner of conveying, as if he should name every one, 'I come to thee, and give thee my body.' Think with ourselves, Now Christ cometh to me; when the minister reacheth the bread and comes to me, think of heavenly bread, and of the gift of Christ to me by means. And can he do it more familiarly? Is it not as if he would say, 'Mary'? And that is the excellency of the sacrament. It conveyeth Christ to all the saints, and to every one in particular, as if he named every one. And what an encouragement is this to answer again, to open our hearts to receive him, together with the elements! to embrace Christ, join with Christ, and then to keep him when we have him! Do not lose him. He will not be so dealt withal. Remember the covenant we have made to him. I beseech you, let these sweet considerations of Christ dwell in us, and work on every one of our hearts. If they do good on us here on earth, if we by faith lay hold on him, and have intercourse with him, what will it be in the day of judgment! How comfortable will it be to hear him say to every one in particular, 'Come thou, and thou, stand on my right hand, sit and judge the world with me'? (1 Cor. 6:2). Doth he know our names now on earth, and giveth to every one particularly by himself, if we come worthily? and will not he know us then? Oh, that is far more worth than the world's good, to know us then and to call us by our names! Therefore, I beseech you, be acquainted with Christ. Have intercourse, all we can, with him in the word and sacraments, and never rest till we find this sweet result in the use of the means, 'that he is ours, and we are his'.

Beware of formality

Take heed therefore in these times, desperately addicted to formality and popery. I say, take heed, we do depend not upon any outward thing, but look to Christ in all his ordinances, look to the Spirit. All God's children, the church of the first-born, they are θεοδιδακτος [theodidaktos], such as are 'taught of God'. Who can take away the opposite disposition of man's nature to goodness, but God by his Spirit? Who can shine into the soul, and quicken the soul, but Christ by his Spirit? Who is above the heart and conscience, but Christ by his Spirit? Therefore take heed of formality; submit your hearts to the great prophet of the church, that Moses speaketh of (Deut. 18:18), who shall be the great teacher of the church; lift up our hearts to him, that he would teach our hearts, and remove the natural disposition that is in us; that he would 'take off the veil from our hearts', and teach not only what to do, but teach the very doing of them. Teach us to hate what is ill, teach us to believe, and to resist all Satan's temptations. Who can teach but the great teacher, whose chair is in heaven? Therefore take heed of depending on formal things. Lift your hearts to God,

that he would join his teaching with all other teach-
ings. This cannot be too much stood upon. I beseech
you, therefore, take it to heart.

A particular interest in Christ

Give me leave, therefore, to add a few things more.
If Christ speaketh in general to Mary, she answereth
in general; and when he speaks aloof to her, she
answereth aloof to him, afar off, and never gave
him a direct answer, till he gave a direct word to her.
When he said, 'Mary', she gave him a direct answer,
'Rabboni'; not before. I beseech you, therefore, let us
not rest in general promises and the general graces,
that be so much stood on by some, that God hath
a like respect to all. Trust not to that. We must not
enter into his secrets, but let us obey his precepts and
commandments. And withal remember this, when
we hear of a general mercy and commandment for
all nations to believe, and that Christ came to save a
world of sinners, alas! what is that to me, unless thou
by thy Holy Spirit speakest to my soul, and sayest in
particular, 'I am thy salvation', and speakest familiarly
to my soul? Generals are in some degrees comfortable.
But if I find not particular interest by the witness of thy
Holy Spirit to my soul, if thou sayest not to my soul,
'I am thine, and thou art mine', all is to little purpose.
Therefore in the desires of our souls in prayer, let us
desire the Lord to reveal himself in particular. We trust
too much in generals. God is merciful, and Christ came

to redeem the world. They be truths, and good foundations for to found faith upon, but they will not do the deed, till by daily prayer we seek to the Lord, that he would in a particular manner reveal himself to us. This doth Paul pray for (Eph. 1:17), 'that God would vouchsafe to them the Spirit of revelation'. And this is the office of the Holy Spirit. His special office is, to reveal to everyone in particular his estate and condition God-ward. The Holy Ghost knoweth the secrets in the breast of God, and in our own hearts.[1] Now the Holy Ghost can reveal the particular love that lieth in God's breast to our particular souls. And therefore we should desire God, that the Holy Spirit may be sent to seal to us our particular salvation, and never be quiet till we be sealed in particular assurance, that we be they whom Christ came to save. This we ought to labour for. If we labour for it, we shall have it some time or other, for God loveth to be familiar with his children. He loveth not to be strange to them, if they seek his love, but to reveal himself first or last. And few seek it, but God revealeth himself by his Spirit to them before they die; if he doth not, they are sure of it in heaven. And therefore they that be against particulars, they are enemies to their own salvation. Mary regarded not, while Christ spake of generals, but when he came to particulars, then 'Rabboni', and not before.

[1] In margin here, '*Spiritus Dei, et Dei et hominis secreta cognoscit.*' — G. Latin: 'The Spirit of God knows the secret things of both God and mankind.' — P.

Christ's prohibition

'Jesus saith unto her, Touch me not; I am not yet ascended to my Father,' etc.

This verse containeth Christ's prohibition, or Christ's commission or charge. His prohibition, 'Touch me not'; and his reason, 'for I am not yet ascended to my Father'.

His charge, 'Go to my brethren'; and then directeth what to say to them: 'I ascend to my Father, and your Father; to my God, and your God.'

The words be very natural, and need no breaking up to you. But I shall handle them, as they follow one another.

'Jesus said to her, Touch me not.'

'Touch me not.' Why? He would have Thomas not only touch, but to put his finger into his side; that is more than touching him (John 20:27). But our Saviour's intent is to meet with a disposition in Mary something carnal, something low and mean, in regard of this glorious occasion, Christ being now risen and glorified, for his resurrection was the first degree of his glorification. And therefore, 'Touch me not.' She came with too much a carnal mind to touch him, when she said, 'Rabboni'. It was not satisfaction enough for her to answer, 'Rabboni', but she runneth to him, and claspeth him, and clingeth about him, as the affection of love did dictate to her. But saith he, 'Touch me not' in such a manner. This is not a fit manner for thee to touch me in, now I am risen again. In a word, she had thought to converse with Christ in as familiar a manner as before, when she poured ointment on his head. He was the same person, but the case is altered. That was in the days of his humiliation; now he was risen again, and it was the first degree of his glorification. There was another manner of converse due to him; and therefore, 'Touch me not.' Thou thinkest to touch me as thou didst before, but thou must not do it. She was too much addicted to his bodily presence.

Outward things

1. *It is that that men will labour after, and have laboured for, even from the beginning of the world,* to be too much addicted to present things, and to sense. They will worship Christ, but they must have a picture before them. They will adore Christ, but they must bring his body down to a piece of bread; they must have a presence. And so instead of raising their hearts to God and Christ in a heavenly manner, they pull down God and Christ to them. This the pride and base earthliness of man will do. And therefore saith Christ, 'Touch me not' in that manner; it is not with me now as it was before. We must take heed of mean and base conceits of Christ. What saith Paul (2 Cor 5:16)? 'I know no man now, according to the flesh; no, not Christ himself, now he is risen.' Christ was of such a tribe, stature, had such gifts and qualities. What is that to me? Christ is now Lord of lords, and King of kings. He is glorious in heaven, and so I conceive of him: 'I know no man after the flesh; no, not Christ himself.' I forget what he was

on earth, and think of him what he is now in heaven. Therefore to bring him down to our base conceits, to sense, and the like, this is the humour of men that labour to cross the scope of the gospel. For why are men so addicted to outward things, outward compliments? It is pride, it is satanical pride. They think that God is delighted with whatsoever their folly is delighted withal. Because amongst men there must be a deal a-doing, therefore they think God is well pleased with such things. God is a Spirit, and though outward things be necessary, yet all must not be turned outward, as in popery. We must not bring God down to our foolish conceits, as if he were delighted as we are (Josh. 4:24).

2. *It is wonderful easy too.* All outward things, any naughty[1] men have them with their sins.[2] Let a man perform a little outward compliment, he may be what he will be, let him live as he will, and be possessed that outward things will serve the turn. He is safe; his conscience is daubed up, till God by sense of wrath awakeneth conscience; and then they shall find it another matter to deal with God than by compliment.

3. *There is also a great glory in outward things.* There is commendations, and men's observance of them, as in the Pharisees, and in popery. But the spiritual worship of Christ hath no observance to the eye of the world. It is between God and the soul. Men naturally love those

[1] That is, 'wicked'.—G.

[2] In margin here, '*Externa Deo placere nequeunt.*'—G. Latin: 'External things cannot please God.'—P.

things that be glorious. It is said of Ephraim, that he loved to tread out the corn, but not to plough (Hos. 10:11); that is, Ephraim will take that which is easy, but not that in God's worship which is hard. There be two things in God's service: an easy thing, which is outward compliment; an hard thing, which is to trust him, to deny ourselves, to rely upon him and live by faith.[1] And that Ephraim will not do. Ephraim will tread the corn, because the heifer may eat corn; but there be hard things in religion which he will not practise. He will not plough. 'Touch me not', saith Christ. Thou hast not conceits spiritual enough to deal with me, now I am risen.

But what is the reason? 'Touch me not; *for* I am not yet ascended to my Father.' That seemeth to be a strong reason. But it seemeth to be a contrary reason. Touch me not now, when my body is present; but touch me when I am gone, and removed out of sight of all flesh. Touch me not now, when thou mayest touch me; and touch me when there is an impossibility of touching me. This is seemingly strange. But indeed there is no contrariety in it: 'Touch me not; *for* I am not yet ascended to the Father.'

There is a double meaning of the words. First of all, 'Touch me not; for I am not yet ascended', *etc.* Thou needest not clasp and cling about me, as if I would stay

---

[1] In margin here, '*Arduum et difficile est in fide vivere.*' — G. Latin: : 'It is a hard and difficult thing to live by faith.' — P.

no more with you below; 'I am not yet ascended to the Father.' There will be time enough afterwards. For the word 'touch', in the original, doth not signify merely to touch, but clasp, associate, join, and solder with a thing.[1] The Scripture speaking of the evil man, you shall not touch him; that is, not make him one with him. The devil shall not take him from Christ and make him one with himself. It is a strange word in the original: 'Thou claspest about me, thou dost more than touch me, thou clingest to me and wilt not leave me, as if I would go presently to the Father; but I am not yet ascended to the Father.' That is one part of the meaning.

But there is a farther than that, 'I am not yet ascended to the Father; touch me not.' That is, it is another manner of touch that I look for – better for thee, and in some regard for me – to touch me by the hand of faith when I am ascended to the Father. Then touch me, and take thy full of touching me. But for the present I am not ascended; I have not done all; I have not manifested myself to my disciples in full. When I am ascended, all is done, and then there is place for touch. And that I take is meant here, I am not yet ascended to the Father. Thou thinkest I have done all that is to be done, but thou art deceived. I must ascend to the Father, and when I am there I expect to be touched after another manner,

[1] In margin here, '*Non solum significat tangere, sed adhaerere, conglutinari*, Isa. 52:11; 2 Cor. 6:17. *A tabernaculo impiorum hominum recedite*, Num. 16:27.'—G. Latin: 'Draw back from the tent of the wicked.'—P.

after a gracious, spiritual manner, which is by faith; as Augustine saith well, 'Send up thy faith to heaven, and then thou touchest Christ.'[1] As he said in the sacrament, '*Quid paras dentem et ventrem? Crede, et manducasti*: What dost thou prepare thy teeth and stomach for? Believe, and thou hast eaten.'[2] So the best communion with Christ is to believe, till we come to heaven to have eternal communion with him. This touch will do thee little good, and it pleaseth me as little. When I am ascended to the Father, then touch me at the full. So you see what Christ meaneth.

The life of a Christian here, and the manner of the dispensation of Christ here, is by promise, and by his Spirit; that we should live by faith, and not by sense. The life of sight is reserved for another world, when we are fitted for it. She was not fit for a life of sense, but was to expect the Holy Ghost from heaven; to be filled with that, and then to be filled with faith and love; and then to have an holy communion with him in heaven. But 'I am not yet ascended.' Thus you see the meaning, 'Touch me not.'

There be two reasons of Christ's prohibition.

1. *Her respects were too carnal and ordinary*, considering he was in the state of glory. And then,

---

[1] In margin here, '*Mitte fidem in coelum et tetigisti.*' — G.

[2] For the first part of this reference see Com. or Hom. on Matt. 9:21; for the latter, cf. Tract 26 in Joan; e.g., '*Credere in Christian hoc est manducare vivum*'; also in John Evang. c. vi. — G.

2. *For that there will be time enough.* Do not stand embracing of me, there is a greater work for thee to do. Christ preferred the great work of giving notice to his disciples of his resurrection, before the office of respect and service to himself. Go about a duty, that I more regard a great deal: 'Go, tell my brethren I ascend', *etc.* So that every part of the text yields satisfaction to that prohibition.

Christ's commission

'Go', saith he, 'to my brethren.' I have another work for thee to do, 'Touch me not.' Thou clasps about me as if thou hadst nothing to do. There is another work to do that pleaseth me better, and more fit for thee: to comfort them that are in distress, my poor brethren and disciples. And therefore 'Go to my brethren, and say unto them.' So that Christ prefers a work of charity to his poor disciples before a work of compliment to his own person. She clingeth about him; but 'this is not it I would have'. Those poor souls are mourning and disconsolate for me, as if I were clean taken away; go to them, and prevent their farther sorrow.

God hath a wonderful respect to others. It is strange that Christ should say, 'Go and be reconciled to thy brethren, and then offer thy sacrifice' (Matt. 5:24). As if he would have his own sacrifice neglected, rather than we should not be reconciled to others. And so a work of charity and love is preferred before an *officium*[1] and

---

[1] Latin: duty. —P.

compliment to himself. Let us show our love to the first table in the second, our love to God by our love to man. Everything hath its measure and time. Away therefore with this over-much embracing and touching. Go thy way, thou hast another work to do: 'Go to my brethren.' And so you see, as I take it, the full meaning of the words.

Observe the circumstances. Who must go? Here is a commission and command. And to whom? To the disciples of Christ. And when doth Christ bid her go? When he was risen, and in the first estate of glory. What is the message? 'Tell my brethren I am ascending to my Father, and your Father; to my God, and your God.' It is worth your considering a little.

1. *Who is sent?* A woman. A woman to be the apostle of apostles, to be the teacher of the great teachers in the world. Mary Magdalene was sent to instruct the apostles in the great articles of Christ's resurrection and ascension to heaven. By a woman death came into the world, and by a woman life was preached to the apostles; because indeed she was more affectionate, and affection taketh all. And that makes that sex more addicted to religion, by the advantage of their affection; for religion is merely a matter of affection. Though it must have judgment shine before it, yet it is specially in the heart and affections. And she had showed a great deal of affection. She stood out when the rest went away (John 19:25). She was constant, and broke through all

difficulties; and then God honoured her to be the first preacher of his resurrection.

God's course is to trust secrets in earthen vessels, that earthen vessels should carry heavenly treasure; and therefore stick not at the vessel, but look to the treasure (2 Cor. 4:7). A woman may teach the greatest apostle. Look not to the man, but to the message. Elijah will not refuse the meat because the raven brought it (1 Kings 17:4). And a condemned man will not refuse a pardon, because a mean man bringeth it. Take off pride in spiritual respects. When God honours any man to bring news of reconciliation, stoop to him, of what condition soever he be.

2. *To whom must she go?* 'Go, tell *my brethren*', the apostles. Go to the apostles, that are disconsolate men, now orphans, deprived of their Master and Lord. Disconsolate men, and not in vain, so not without cause; for they had reason to be discomforted, not only for their want of Christ, but for their own ill carriage towards Christ. One of them denieth him, and the rest forsake him; and yet 'my brethren', 'go tell my brethren'.

3. *When did he speak this?* After his resurrection, in the state of glory; in the beginning of it, and when he is ascending to heaven; and yet he owneth them as brethren, though such brethren as had dealt most unbrotherly with him.

Christ our brother

But how came they to be his brethren? And how come we to be Christ's brothers? Christ is the first-born of many brethren (Rom. 8:29). He is the Son of God by nature; and all others now, by grace and adoption (Rom. 8:17). Christ is the *primo-genitus*[1] amongst many brethren; and in Christ we have one Father with Christ. We have one honour, and we shall be all kings and heirs of heaven, as he is. 'If sons, then heirs' (Gal. 4:7); the apostle makes the coherence. Now we are all in Christ sons of God, heirs with him. To go to the condition of nature that he took, our nature; and therefore having our flesh, he is our brother (Heb. 2:14). The very reprobate may say so. Yet that is a ground of comfort, that he is a man as we are. But that is not the main thing considerable. He is our brother in a spiritual respect, in regard of adoption. He is the first Son of God, and we in him sons. He is the first heir of God, and we in him are heirs. And therefore 'go to my brethren'.

Beloved, it is a point of marvellous comfort, that Christ was not ashamed to call them brethren (Psa. 22:22): 'I will declare thy name amongst my brethren,' saith Christ. Our Saviour Christ alluded to that psalm in this passage; and so it is read (Heb. 2:12), out of that psalm. Christ hath taken all relations, that are comfortable, upon him towards us. 'He is the everlasting Father, the Prince of peace' (Isa. 9:6).

[1] first-born.—P.

He is 'a second Adam', and therefore a father in that regard. The first Adam is the father of all that perish; the second Adam is the father of all that shall be saved. As he is our brother, so our husband. He could not be our husband, except he were our brother. He must take our nature, and be one with us, before we can be one with him. He is our friend. Before this time he called them friends, as you see in John: 'I will call you friends' (John 15:15). But here is a sweeter term, 'brethren'. There is no relation that hath any comfort in it, but Christ hath taken it on him. He is our head, husband, friend, father, brother, and whatsoever can convey comfort to us.[1] And the truth of it is, he is these things more truly than any relation is made true on earth. For these relations of husband and wife, and brother and sister, and father and child, are but shadows of that everlasting relation that Christ hath taken upon him; the reality and truth itself is in Christ. We think there is no brother, but the brother in flesh; no father, but the father in flesh. Alas! these are but shadows, and quickly cease: 'the fashion of the world passeth away' (1 Cor. 7:31). Brother is another relation, whereof these are but shadows. These do but represent the best things that are in heaven. Christ is the father, brother, friend, and whatsoever is comfortable in heaven; therefore 'go tell my brethren'.

---

[1] In margin here, '1 Cor. xi. 3; 1 Cor. xii. 27; Eph. v. 23; 1 John ii. 2, *seq.*; Rev. xxii. 3, *seq.*'—G.

Obj. Ay, but saith the poor soul, I that have been so sinful, so unworthy a wretch, shall I have comfort in this, that Christ is my brother, and I am Christ's? I cannot do it.

Ans. I profess thou canst not do it, 'flesh and blood must not teach it thee', thou must be taught by the Spirit of Christ. But consider how the apostles used Christ. Thou canst not call Christ brother, because thou hast been a sinner, and hast carried thyself unkindly to Christ. And did not the disciples so? Did not they leave him, and one of them deny him, and that with oaths? Therefore, whatsoever our sins have been, deny not our relation to Christ. The poor prodigal said, 'I am not worthy to be called a son', I am not worthy to be called a servant (Luke 15:21). He denied not that he was a son, but he was unworthy of it. And so I am unworthy to be a spouse and brother of Christ, yet do not our unfaithful hearts so much pleasure, as to deny our relation.

The apostles were so dignified, as to be called the 'pillars of the world' (Gal. 2:9). But these left him, and yet for all that, in this time of their desertion of him, 'go tell my brethren'. Therefore be not discouraged. Go to Christ in our worst condition, in our greatest temptations, when our hearts misgive us most that we have used God most unkindly, and Satan plied us most with desperate temptations; yet own him for our brother, who owned his disciples when they dealt most unkindly with him.[1] I beseech you, count it a comfort unvaluable, which no tongue is able to express, that Christ after his resurrection should call 'brethren'. He might well call them brethren after his resurrection, because then all debts were discharged by his death. He had paid their debts, and now the acquittance was due to them, because Christ as surety had paid all. Now I am risen, 'go and tell my brethren so'. If we can make use of the death and resurrection of Christ, and say, Christ hath died for my sins, and rose again for my justification; I will interest myself in his death, I will claim the virtue of his resurrection; then take the comfort of this. In popery, they had much comfort in those dark times, when a company of proud, carnal, beastly men ruled the roost according to their own lusts. These clergymen made a great pother[2] with fraternity and brotherhood. And if they were of such a fraternity of Dominic or Francis, or merely in a friar's cowl, it was not only satisfactory, but meritorious, they could not do amiss. Away with these shadows. Here is the brotherhood that must comfort Christians, that Christ owned us for brethren after his resurrection. He paid dear for it, alas! Are we worth so much, that God should become man to die for us, to rise again for us, to justify us, and make us brethren? That infinite love, that God became man and died for us, and rose again

---

[1] In margin here, '*Tentatio est ad Christum eundi opportunitas, ut nobis succurrat.*'—G. Latin: 'Temptation is an opportunity to go to Christ to seek his help.'—P.

[2] commotion or fuss.—P.

to own us for his brethren, will satisfy all doubts. Shall we doubt anything of that love? When he out of his free love will own us as brethren, shall not we own him? I confess it is a marvellous thing, in times of temptation it is difficult to make use of it. Oh, but pray with the good apostle, 'Lord, increase our faith' (Luke 17:5); with the poor man in the gospel, 'I believe; Lord, help my unbelief' (Mark 9:24). So when any temptation cometh for our unworthiness and our undeserving, then think Christ after his resurrection called his apostles 'brethren', and he will be content to be my brother, if I will believe he died for me, and I will cast myself upon him; therefore away with all doubts.

There be many other observations out of the words.

(1.) *Will you have the first words in estate of glory, his first words after death?* 'Go and tell my brethren.' Think in a desperate extremity, think of the sweet message he sent by Mary Magdalene to his unworthy 'brethren', that he died for, and [had] given his blood to make them his brethren. Think of his free love to you. It is not for your worthiness or unworthiness, but of his own free love, that he came from heaven to take your nature. It is his own free love that he came to die; and therefore conceive not of worthiness nor unworthiness, but consider the command of God to believe; and if we perish, perish there. Cast ourselves on our brother, that will own us in our worst condition. That is the grand use.

(2.) Again, If *God owns us in his glorious condition, shall we be ashamed of the doctrine of Christ, of the children of God, to own them?* What saith Christ? It is a terrible thunderbolt. 'He that is ashamed of me and of my word before men, I will be ashamed of him before my heavenly Father' (Mark 8:38). Take heed of being ashamed to stand out a good cause, in matters of religion. Christ was not ashamed to call us brethren when we were at the worst, and he himself in a glorious condition; he was in glory, and the disciples drooping in consideration of their guilt, that they had forsaken him, and yet 'brethren' still. And shall not we own him, that owneth us in state of glory? How shall we look that he will own us hereafter, when he trusteth us with his cause and glory, and we betray all to pleasure such and such? Can we look Christ in the face with comfort, if we neglect his cause, his truth, and his church?

(3.) Again, Make this use of it, *Christ is our brother, and will not he take our parts?* Absalom was a disobedient son, yet Absalom would not let his sister Tamar be abused; he would be revenged of that. And will Christ suffer his sister, his spouse, his church to be abused long? Nay, will he leave his 'dove, his love, his undefiled one' (Song of Sol. 5:2), where he hath placed all his joy and contentment, to the malice and fury of the enemy long? Certainly he will not. Certainly he will be avenged on his enemies. If nature, that he hath put into the wicked, sinful men, teach them to revenge indignities offered to their kindred, will Christ suffer his brethren, his sisters, to be abused? 'Saul, Saul, why persecutest thou me?' (Acts 9:4). Now he is in heaven, the church's case is his own. And therefore comfort ourselves with that sweet relation. Christ hath undertaken to be our brother in state of glory. What a comfort is it that we have a brother in heaven! What a comfort was it to the poor patriarchs, when they thought with themselves, we have a brother, Joseph, that is the second man in the kingdom! And so, what a great comfort is it for poor Christians to think, that the second in heaven, that sitteth at God's right hand, that is King of kings and Lord of lords, and that ruleth all, is our brother! Is not this a main comfort, yea, beyond all expression, if we could make use of it by faith answerable to our trouble? Therefore go to Joseph, that hath laid up comfort for us. He hath comfort enough for us, he hath treasures of comfort. Whatsoever is necessary for us, we may have in Christ our elder brother. And therefore 'go to my brethren'.

I beseech you, let us make a use of exhortation, to be stirred up, to labour by faith to be one with Christ; and then he will be our head, our husband, our brother, our friend, our all. Say what you can, Christ will be 'all in all' to all his. He hath enough in him: 'Of his fulness we shall receive, and grace for grace.' Oh labour to be one with Christ. Do not lose such a comfort as is offered. He offereth himself first to be our Saviour and Redeemer, and then our brother; never rest therefore till we have part in

Christ. And then labour to make use of, in all temptations catch fast hold of, everything that is useful, as it is the nature of faith to do, like Benhadad's servants, who made use of that word 'brother'. He is my 'brother', said the king of Israel, as common offices make kindred (1 Kings 20:33). He had but let pass the term of 'brother', and they would not let it go, but catch at it: 'Thy brother Benhadad.' We see what wisdom flesh and blood can teach, to make an improvement of any comfort in the world, if by kindred, or office, or any relation in the world, they make use of them. And when we be in Christ, shall not we make use of them, when we be troubled with sense of sin, or in desperate conditions? When Christ calleth us brother, shall not we answer, 'I am thy brother'? Blessed be thy mercy and love, that descended so low as to make me thy brother! I beseech you, let us not lose the comforts we may have in the disciples' being called Christ's brethren, when they were in some sort enemies. But he knew their hearts were sound, and it was but their weakness; therefore let no weakness discourage thee. He will not 'quench the smoking flax, nor break the bruised reed' (Matt. 12:20). Is thy heart right to Christ? art thou not a false hypocrite, a secret traitor to Christ, and to his cause and church? Then be of good comfort; thou mayest go to Christ as to thy brother. Though Peter denied him with his mouth, yet he confessed him with his heart. And therefore 'go tell my disciples', *and Peter* – he hath most guilt, and therefore he hath most need of comfort. Be thy guilt never so great, if thou wilt come into covenant with God, here is mercy for thee, and therefore make this use of it. Never forget, in your worst condition that may be, since Christ will stoop so low to own you to be brethren, to make use of it, if your hearts be right towards him.

The comfort of being Christ's brethren

'Go to my brethren.' Now I come to the commission or charge given to her. 'Go to my brethren.' Who is the party charged? 'Mary.' And what is her charge? To go to the apostles under the sweet term of 'brethren'. When doth he call them so? After his resurrection; when he was in the state of glory. What is the message? It is very sweet, Go, say to them, 'I ascend to my Father, and your Father; to my God, and your God.' 'I ascend'; that is, I presently am to ascend, in a very short time I shall ascend. It was but forty days between Easter and Ascension, and all that time Christ appeared now and then. It is the nature of faith, where it is glorious, for to present future things as if present, especially when they be near. 'I ascend'; that is, I shall very shortly ascend, and it is all one as if I ascend presently. To whom do I ascend? 'I ascend to *my* Father.' To '*my* Father'. That is not comfort enough. Therefore 'to *your* Father too'. 'I ascend to God.' That is not comfort enough. Therefore 'to my God, and your God'. We shall unfold the words as we come at them.

First, Mary Magdalene, a woman, a sinner, is used in the great work of an apostle, to be an apostle to the

43

apostles. I would there were that love in all men to teach what they know; and that humility in others, to be instructed in what they know not. It were a sweet conjunction if it were so. She was a mean person to instruct the great apostles. But, beloved, where there is a great deal of love, there they will teach what they know; and where there is humility, there they will be taught what they know not, though they be never so great. And God will humble the greatest to learn of the meanest sometimes. Therefore he sendeth Mary to the apostles.

I beseech you, in matters of salvation, stand not on terms. Let us take truth from Christ, let us see God and Christ in it, see our own comfort in it, not stand upon persons. Aquila and Priscilla teach the great men knowledge (Acts 18:2, *seq.*). And so it is. Sometimes mean persons are honoured to be instruments of great comforts to persons greater than themselves. She is to go to the apostles under the name of brethren: 'Go tell my brethren.' And she must go to the apostles that were Christ's brethren, and owned to be so now, when he was in glory, when he was risen and exempt from all abasements of the cross and grave, where he was held captive three days under the dominion of sin, when he was freed from all enemies of salvation, and had triumphed over all. 'Go tell my brethren.' So you see there is a sweet affinity and nearness between Christ and his. Christ took our nature on him for this end: he became flesh of our flesh, and bone of our bone, that we spiritually might be flesh of his flesh and bone of his bone. It is no comfort at all; an inducing comfort it is, but no actual, present comfort, that Christ was incarnate for us; for all the world might have comfort in that, Turks, Jews, Pagans, that had the nature of man in them. And all have some comfort in it, as their nature is dignified; and that he took not on him the nature of angels, but the nature of man, his spouse, his church it is that hath the comfort of it. Therefore it is not sufficient that he be bone of our bone and flesh of our flesh; but we must be bone of his bone, and flesh of his flesh. We must be ingrafted and baptised into him by faith, and then the term holdeth, and never till then; so that there is a sweet nearness between Christ and his. 'Brother' is a most comfortable relation. It is a comfort that he took our nature upon him, that God would take 'dust and ashes', earth, into the unity of his person. For God to become man is a great dignifying of man's nature. But to take not only our nature on him, but to take our person particularly near to him; thou and thou to be a member of Christ, there is the honour of it. It induceth us to come to Christ that hath loved our nature so much. But the other is an actual, present comfort, when we can say, 'I am my beloved's, and my beloved is mine.'

Our hearts are too narrow a great deal to embrace the whole comfort that this word affords unto us, that Christ should own us as his brother after his resurrection, for that showeth a reconciliation. 'Brother' is a term of friendship, nay, more than a term of reconciliation, for a man may be reconciled to an enemy; but it is a term of amity, to show that when we believe in Christ and are one with him, our sins are quitted; death is overcome; Satan's head is crushed when God is reconciled. What have they to do with us? They are only to serve our turns to bring us to heaven, and fit us for it. I beseech you, consider of the excellent freedom and dignity of a Christian; his freedom in that he is the brother of Christ; free from all, being owned by Christ after his resurrection, all being quit by his death who was our surety, else he should be in the grave to this day. And then think of our dignity, to be brother to him that is King of heaven, Lord of lords, ruler of the whole world; that hath all things subject to him. Oh that our hearts were enlarged to conceive the wonderful comfort that every Christian hath in this relation! 'Go tell my apostles', under the sweet term of 'brethren'.

Who art thou, will Satan say, flesh and blood, a piece of earth, wretched sot; wilt thou claim kindred of Christ?

Ay, saith the Christian, believing soul, it is true. If it were my own worthiness it were another matter, but I will give him the lie. When he owned me for his brother after his resurrection, shall I deny the relation? Therefore never believe Satan's tempting words and sinful flesh; for Satan cometh to us in our own flesh, and maketh us think God and Christ to be such and such. Ay, but what saith Christ himself? Believe him and not Satan, that cometh to thee in thy own despairing, dark, doubting flesh. Believe the word of Christ, who calleth thee brother, if thou believest on him, and castest thyself upon him.

The dignity of Christ's brethren

This showeth the dignity of a Christian when he is once in Christ, the excellent, superexcellent, transcendent glory of a Christian. When they told our Saviour Christ that his mother and brethren were to speak with him, saith he, 'They that hear my word and do it, they are my brother, and sister, and my mother' (Luke 8:21). This is the excellency of a Christian, that he is of so near a kin to Christ. When we believe Christ, it is all one as if we conceived Christ, as if we were brothers to Christ, as if we were of the nearest kindred to him. Nay, it is more; he preferreth mother before mother, brother before brother; mother in spirit before mother in the flesh, and brother in spirit before all other brothers. Therefore an excellent thing to be a Christian! When once a Christian giveth himself to Christ, and denieth his own doubting, despairing heart, which is the greatest enemy he hath? 1. Then what belongeth to him? Then God is his, and Christ is his; he must have an inheritance; he is fellow-heir without [doubt]; all are his. 2. What carrieth he in him? He carrieth in him the Spirit of the Father and the Son, and the graces of the Spirit, which make him lovely to God. 3. What cometh from him? Having the precious graces of the Holy Ghost in him, what can come from him as a Christian but grace and comfort to others? He is a tree of righteousness; and what can come from a good tree but good fruit? So far he is so.

So if you regard what belongeth to them, what is in them, the inheritance they shall have, or what cometh from a Christian, that is, brother of Christ, he is an excellent person, more excellent than his neighbour. There is no man in the world, never so great, but is a base person in comparison of a Christian. What will all be ere long? If a man be not in Christ, these things will add to our vexation. It will be a misery to have had happiness; the greater will be the misery when they must be parted withal. And therefore raise your hearts to consider of the excellent condition of a Christian when he is once the brother of Christ.

I confess it is an hidden dignity; as Paul saith, 'Our life is *hid* with Christ in God' (Col. 3:3). We have a life, a glorious life, but it is hid. It is dark; sometimes under melancholy, sometimes under temptations, sometimes under the afflictions of the world and disgrace, and so it is an hidden excellency, but it is a true excellency. The world knoweth us not more than they know God and Christ. But, it is no matter, God knoweth us by name. He knew Mary by name, as it is said in Isaiah, 'I have called thee by name' (45:3). He is a shepherd, that knoweth his sheep by name, and is known of them. He knoweth thee, and thee, and thee, by name; yea, and the hairs of thy head are numbered; and therefore it matters not though thy dignities be hid with the world. Yet God knoweth them. He hath written all thy members in a book, and he hath a book of remembrance of thee. And therefore it is no matter though it be an hidden dignity. It is a true dignity to be a brother of Christ.

Let us oppose this to the disgrace of the world, and to all temptations of discouragement whatsoever. What are all discouragements to this? They fall all before this, that we are the sons of God and brethren of Christ. What can discourage a man that is thus apprehensive of this excellency upon good terms? I will enlarge the point no further, but leave it to your own meditations, and the Spirit of God work with it!

Christ's timing

'Go to my brethren.' When doth he bid her go? Now after his resurrection, when he was to ascend to heaven. The first degree of his glory was his resurrection, after his lowest abasement in the grave. You see that honour doth not change Christ's disposition, as it doth amongst men. When they be advanced to great places, they will not look on their old friends and acquaintance; but Christ hath no such disposition, he owneth his poor disciples in their greatest abasements: 'Go tell my brethren.' Now when he was in a state of glory, ready to go to heaven, and he giveth them a more comfortable title now than ever before. In the gospel he called them 'servants', and 'friends', and 'apostles', and 'disciples'; but now 'brethren', a word of all sweetness, and nothing but sweetness. 'Go tell my brethren' presently; Christ would have no delay, for he saw they had present need. Christ's love is a quickening love, and the fruits of it are very speedy. There is more than angelical swiftness in Christ when there is need of him. God helpeth at need, in the most seasonable time, and he knoweth the time best of all. He did but rise in the morning, and the very same day, 'Go tell my brethren.' Ye have (Song of Sol. 2:8), that Christ cometh 'leaping upon the mountains'. When he was to help his church, 'he leaped over the mountains'; as in the eighth verse, 'The voice of my beloved! behold, he cometh leaping upon the mountains, skipping upon the hills.' He cometh from heaven to earth, from earth to the grave; and now he is risen, he is all in haste, he maketh no stay, because his manner of despatch is, to help and comfort by the ministry of others. Go quickly; do not stand embracing of me, but 'go and tell my brethren'.

Obj. But why then do not we find comfort sooner, that are afflicted?

Ans. Beloved, where is the fault? Is it in Christ? You stand out at staves-end[1] with Christ; you will not embrace comforts when they be offered, or else you be not sufficiently humbled; for he is wise as he is swift, he knoweth which be the best times.

You see then that Christ, so soon as ever it is fit for him, he will come. If he should come sooner, he would come too soon; if afterward, it would be too late. He is

---

[1] That is, at a distance, or on ceremony. — G.

the best discerner of times and seasons that can be, and therefore wait his leisure. If thou want comfort, humble soul, whosoever thou art, wait his leisure. Certainly he knoweth the best time, and when the time is come, he will come. 'He that will come shall come' (Heb. 10:37), there is no question of that.

Christ's love constant and invincible

Now as he sent her in all haste, preferring it before any compliment to his own person, so it is a constant love. As it is a quick love that God bears to his children, so it is a constant, invincible love. They had dealt most unbrotherly with him, for everyone had forsaken him, and Peter had denied him; yet, 'Go tell my brethren.' One would think this water would have quenched this fire; this unkind and unbrotherly dealing would have quenched this love in Christ's breast. It is true, if it had been the mere love of man, it had been something; but it was the love of an infinite person, that took our nature out of love, and therefore it was a constant and invincible love. Nothing could conquer it, not the thoughts of their unkind dealings, no, not their denying and forsaking of him. But still, 'Go tell my brethren.' 'Love is strong as death' (Song of Sol. 8:6). Death could not hold Christ in the grave, but love held him on the cross. When he came to the work of our redemption, love then held him on earth; but when he was in the grave, it brake through all there. Indeed, it was stronger than death, in Christ.

Quest. Why is Christ's love so constant, so invincible, that nothing can alter it?

Resolution. The ground of it is, it is free love. He fetcheth the ground of his love from his own heart; not from our worthiness or unworthiness, but from his own freedom, and God's eternal purpose. God hath purposed to save so many, and those and no more he giveth to Christ to save. And God looketh on his own purpose, Christ's free love, and that is the ground of all. And therefore whom he loveth he loveth to the end, because he looked on us in his election. The Lord knoweth who are his; the foundation is so sure, if once we be God's we are ever God's.[1] For Christ looks on us in God's election. Therefore, if ever he showeth his love to us, once his love and for ever his love. If anything in man could hinder it, it would have hindered it at our first conversion, when we were at worst, even enemies; if nothing could hinder it then, what can hinder it afterwards? as the apostle reasoneth strongly: (Rom. 5:10), if we be reconciled by his death, much more will he save us by his life. 'If when we were enemies we were reconciled to God by the death of his Son, now much more, being reconciled, shall we be saved by his life?' If when we had no goodness, but opposition and rebellion in us, we were saved by his death, Christ is much more able to save us now by his life, triumphing over death and being glorious in the heavens.

[1] In margin here, '*Fundamenta tamen stant inconcussa Syonis.*' — G. Latin (poetic): 'Nevertheless the foundation of Zion stands firm.' — P.

Obj. Oh but, saith the poor soul, I am a poor weak creature, and ready to fall away every day.

Ans. Ay but Christ's love is constant. 'Whom he loveth he loveth to the end.' What saith the apostle? (Rom. 8:38, 39), 'Neither things present, nor things to come, shall be able to separate us from the love of Christ'; and therefore be strong in the Lord, and in the power of his might; do not trust to yourselves, nor trouble yourselves for things to come. If you be free from guilt of former sins, never question time to come. God is unchangeable in his nature, unchangeable in his love. He is 'Jehovah, I am', always; not 'I was or will be', but 'I am always'. If ever he loved thee, he will love thee for ever. You see the constancy of Christ's love, 'Go tell my brethren.' Now when they had most deeply offended him, they were renegadoes, having all left him; and then when he had most need of their comfort, being in greatest extremity; and yet 'Go tell my brethren.'

Beloved, let us not lose the comfort of the constancy and immutability of Christ's love. Let us conceive that all the sweet links of salvation are held on God's part strong, not on ours; the firmness is on God's part, not on ours. Election is firm on God's part, not on ours. We choose indeed as he chooseth us, but the firmness is of his choosing; so he calleth us, we answer, but the firmness is of his action. He justifieth; we are made righteous, but the firmness is of his imputation. Will he forgive sins today, and bring us into court and damn us tomorrow? No. The firmness is of his action. We are ready to run into new debts every day, but whom he justifieth he will glorify. The whole chain so holdeth, that all the creatures in heaven and earth cannot break a link of it. Whom he calleth he will justify and glorify. Therefore never doubt of continuance, for it holds firm on God's part, not thine. God embraceth us in the arms of his everlasting love, not that we embraced him first. When the child falleth not, it is from the mother's holding the child, and not from the child's holding the mother. So it is God's holding of us, knowing of us, embracing of us, and justifying of us that maketh the state firm, and not ours; for ours is but a reflection and result of his, which is unvariable. The sight of the sun varieth, but the sun in the firmament keepeth always his constant course. So God's love is as the sun, invariable, and for ever the same. I only touch it, as the foundation of wonderful comfort, which they undermine that hold the contrary.

Christ's love to his cast down brethren

The next point is, that Christ chose Mary to go tell his brethren, and under the sweet title of 'brethren', to deliver this sweet message, 'I am going to my Father, and your Father; to my God, and your God.' He telleth them the sweetest words in the worst times.

This point differeth from the former thus. The former was, that Christ's love is constant, and always the same. But now Christ most showeth his love when we are most cast down: in the worst times, if our casting down be with repentance. He never said 'brethren' before, but reserved the term of 'brethren' for the worst time of all. The sweetest discoveries of Christ are in the worst times of all to his children. Mothers will bring out anything to their children, that is sweet and comfortable to them, in their sickness. Though they frowned on them before, yet the exigency of the child requires it. When there is need, anything cometh out that may please the child. The poor disciples were not only in affliction, being the scorn of the world, the shepherd being smitten and the sheep scattered, but their inward grief was greater. They were inwardly confounded and ashamed to see Christ come to such an end. They were full of unbelief. Though Christ had told them he would rise again, they could not believe; and so what with fear, and what with doubt, and what with grief for their using of Christ so unkindly and leaving him, certainly they were in a perplexed and disconsolate condition; yet now, 'Go and tell my brethren.'

We see, then, that after relapses, when we be in state of grace, to deal unkindly with Christ, must needs be matter of grief and shame; yet if we be humbled for it and cast down, even then Christ hath a sweet message for us by his Holy Spirit: 'Go, tell my brethren.' In the Song of Solomon, the church, the spouse of Christ, had dealt unkindly with Christ, by losing him and forsaking him (chap. 3:1-5). In the third chapter, she had lost him, and sought him on her bed, but found him not. She rose, and went to the watchmen, and then went through the city, but found him not. At length she found him whom her soul loved. Then Christ speaks most sweetly and comfortably to her in the beginning of the fourth chapter, but especially in the sixth chapter, after she had dealt most unkindly with Christ. He standeth at the door knocking and waiting, till his locks dropped with rain, in resemblance of a lover that standeth at the door, and is not suffered to come in. Afterwards he leaveth her for this unkindness, yet not so, but that there was some sweet relish left upon the door. God always leaveth something in his children to long after him; and at length, after much longing, Christ manifesteth himself sweetly to her (chap. 6:4, 5), and breaketh out, 'Thou art beautiful, O my love, as Tirzah, comely as Jerusalem, terrible as an army with banners; turn away thine eyes from me, for they have overcome me; thy hair is as a flock of goats', *etc.*, and so goeth on, 'My love, my dove, my undefiled one.' He could not satisfy himself in the commendations of his church, being, as it were, overcome with love. And this showeth, that after we have dealt unkindly with Christ, and our consciences are ashamed and abashed with it, as it is fit they should, yet if we will wait a while, and be content, nor be desperate, nor yield to temptation, if we stay but a while, Christ will manifest himself to us, and show that he valueth and prizeth the hidden graces we cannot see. He can see gold in ore. He can see hidden love, and hidden faith and grace, that we cannot see in temptations; and he will manifest all at length, and show his love when we stand most in need of it. We see it in David, who was deeply humbled for his folly with Bathsheba, for there was not one, but many sins, as murder and adultery, *etc.*; yet being now humbled, God sent him and Bathsheba wise Solomon, to succeed him in his kingdom. He forgetteth all; and so you see our Saviour Christ forgetteth all their unkindness. He biddeth her not 'Go, tell my renegade disciples, that owned not me; they care not for me: I care not for them; I am above death and all, and now will use them as they did me.' Oh no. But 'Go, tell my brethren', without mentioning anything that they have done unkindly.

What is the reason? It is sufficient to a gracious soul that it is thus; it is the course of God. But there be reasons to give satisfaction.

Reason 1. First, *The love of Christ to a poor, disconsolate, afflicted soul is most seasonable.* When they have relapsed and dealt unkindly with Christ, then Christ not only forgiveth, but forgets all; nay, and calleth them under the term of 'brethren', which is more than forgiving or forgetting. Oh now it is seasonable. For there is a wonderful dejection of spirit after unkind usage of Christ, in a soul that knows what Christ means. It is as a shower of rain after great drought. It falleth weighty upon the soul.

Reason 2. Secondly, *The freedom of Christ's love most appeareth then, when no desert of ours can move it.* For is not that love free, when we have dealt unkindly with him, and joined with the world and with the flesh, and dealt slipperily with him, that then he would speak kindly to us and make love to us? Lord, if I had had my due, what would have become of me? If he had sent them word according to their deserts, he might have said, 'Go, tell the apostate, base people that have dealt unworthily with me, whom I will send to hell.' Oh no. But 'tell my brethren'. His free love appeareth most at such times, when our souls are most dejected.

Reason 3. Thirdly, *Satan roareth then most, then he most of all showeth his horns, when we are relapsed.* Oh, saith he, if thou hadst never found kindness, it had been something; but thou hast dealt unworthily that hast had so many favours, and dost thou so requite the Lord of glory? Now this love of Christ doth exceedingly confound Satan, and trouble his plots. He knoweth then that God leaveth men, and he joineth with a guilty conscience, and a guilty conscience maketh them to fear all they have deserved, Shall I look God in the face, and Christ in the face when I have used them thus? Shall I receive the sacrament and join with God's people? Now Satan doth join with guilt of conscience, and carrieth it further; and when God seeth them dejected and humbled for this, he speaketh more comfort to them than ever before.

There is none of us all, I can except none, but had need of this. Have we dealt so unkindly with Christ since our conversion? Have not we dealt proudly, and unkindly, and carelessly with him? And if we have the love of Christ in our breasts, it will shame and abash us. Now if we have joined with a temptation, Satan will say, Will you go to God, and to prayer, that have served God thus? Shall I yield to this temptation? If we can shame ourselves and say, Lord, I take all shame to myself, I have dealt most unworthily with thee, we shall hear a voice of comfort presently. And therefore whatsoever our conditions be, be invited to repentance, though thou hast fallen and fallen again. 'I have dealt unkindly.' Did not Peter so? and yet, 'Go, tell my disciples, and tell Peter.' The pope will have him head of the church. I am sure he was head in forsaking of Christ, and indeed Christ ever upbraided Peter with forsaking of him. Now only he biddeth him feed, feed, feed, that he might take more notice of it; but he was so kind that he never cast it into his teeth (John 21:15-17).

Obj. But saith the poor drooping soul, If I had never tasted of mercy it had been something.

Ans. But object not that, for though Peter's offence was great, yet his repentance was great; and though thy sins be great, yet if thy repentance and humiliation be answerable, thou shalt have most comfort of all. And therefore let no man be discouraged.

If we go on in sinful, desperate courses, as the fashion of the world is, speak what we can, if we speak out our lungs, many will not leave an oath, nor their profane base courses and filthy ways; ill they have been already, and ill they will be till they come to hell. Some such there be, but better we are to speak too. Whosoever thou art, that are weary of thy profane, base, godless courses, be humbled for them. When thou art humbled and broken-hearted, then think of Christ, as he offers himself; think of nothing but love, nothing but mercy. Satan will picture him thus and thus, but when thou beest humbled and broken-hearted, he is readier to entertain thee than thou art to fly to him. And therefore at such times consider how Christ offereth himself to thee. He that died for his enemies, and seeks them that never sought him, that is found of them that sought him not, will he refuse them that seek him? If thou hast an heart humbled, and hast a desire of favour, will he refuse thee, that receiveth many in the world? Therefore do not despair. We as ambassadors beseech you, saith the apostle. Thou desirest God's favour and Christ's love. Thou desirest them, and Christ entreateth thee, and then thou art well met. Thou wouldst fain have pardon and mercy, so would Christ fain bestow it upon thee. Therefore join not to Satan. Take heed of temptations in such a case as this is. Take heed of refusing our own mercies. When God offers mercy in the bowels of his compassion, refuse it not. Christ is ready to show great kindness in our greatest unkindness, if we be humbled for it.

But this belongeth to those that be broken-hearted, that can prize and value Christ. They that go on in presumptuous courses shall find Christ in another manner of majesty. They shall find him as a judge whom they despised as a brother; and they that will not come in and subject themselves to his mercy, they shall find his justice. If they will not come under this sceptre, they shall find his rod of iron to crush them to pieces. And therefore let no corrupt, careless person, that will go on, fortify their presumption from hence. It belongeth only to them to be humbled and abased with the sight of sin, and consideration of their unkindness and unworthy dealing with Christ. I know such as are most subject to discouragement, and Satan is most ready to close with them in strong temptations above all. Oh, but never let them despair, but consider what the apostle saith: 'While sin aboundeth, grace aboundeth much more' (Rom. 5:20). If there be height, depth, and breadth of sin in us, there is now more height, and depth, and breadth of mercy in Christ; yea, more than we can receive.

I have fallen from God, saith the soul. What if thou hast? but God is not fallen from thee. Peter denied Christ, but did Christ deny Peter? No. Christ hath not denied thee. What saith the Lord in Jeremiah? 'Will the husband take the wife when she hath been naught? no; yet return to me, O Israel' (Jer. 3:1). But say, thou hast been false, and committed such and such sins; whatsoever they be, though adultery, yet return to me.

Quest. Oh, but is it possible God should do it?

Resol. Yea, it is possible with him: 'His thoughts are not as thy thoughts; his thoughts are as far above thine as heaven is above earth' (Isa. 55:8, 9).

Obj. Why, no man will do it.

Ans. Ay, but here is the mercy of a God, 'I am God, and not man'; therefore his comforts fail not. If he were so, he would not regard one that hath been so unkind; but he is God, and not man.

The matter of Christ's commission

'Go to my brethren.' I come now to the matter of the commission. Tell them, 'I ascend to my Father, and your Father; to my God, and your God,' which is all included in 'brethren'; for if we be God's in Christ, then God is our Father. But we must not deal in few words with disconsolate souls, but come again and again with the same words. As how many times have you the comfort of the Messiah in Isaiah and the rest of the prophets, again and again? Our hearts are so prone to doubt of God's mercy, of Christ's love, especially after guilt, that all is little enough; and therefore our Saviour studieth to speak sweetly to the heart, 'Go, tell my brethren.' That which a carnal heart and curious[1] head would count tautology and superfluity of words, a gracious heart thinks to be scantiness. Oh, more of that still; I have not enough! This is the pride of men, that will have all things to satisfy the curious ear; but a gracious heart hath never enough. And therefore Christ addeth comfort to comfort: 'Go, tell my brethren, I ascend to my Father, and their Father; to my God, and their God.' The message itself is Christ's ascension. The place

[1] That is, 'over-curious'. — G.

whither is to the Father, a common Father to him and them. Every word hath comfort.

Christ's ascension and ours
'I ascend.'

I ascend to the Father, and to my Father and your Father too. Now I have quitted myself of death, and sin imputed to me as a surety, and I am going to heaven to make an end of all there: 'I ascend to God, to my God and to your God.' We have all one common Father, and one common God.

First, For his ascension. He did not yet ascend. Why then doth he speak for the present? 'I ascend'; that is, I am shortly so to do. And it was in his mind, it was certainly so to be; and therefore he speaks of it in present. It is the phrase of faith, to speak of things to come as if they were present. Faith makes them so to the soul, for it looketh on the word and all things as they are in that Word, who will make good whatsoever he saith. And therefore it is the evidence of things that are not yet, yet they be evident to a faithful soul. If we could learn this aright, to make things to come present, what kind of people should we be! Could we think of our resurrection and ascension and glory to come as present, they would be present to our faith; the things present, or sense, could not withdraw us. If we could set hell before us, could the pleasures of hell bewitch us? If the time to come were present, could anything in the world withdraw us? It could not be. And therefore it is an excellent skill of faith to set things to come before us as present.

He ascendeth. He implieth that he was risen. That was past, and therefore he nameth it not. All Christ's mind was on ascending. Those that are risen together with Christ, their mind is all on ascension, all on heaven. And this is one main reason, because where anything is imperfect, there the spirit resteth not till it attaineth to that perfection that it is destinated unto. When anything hath a proper element and place where it must rest, it resteth not till it be in its own proper place and element. The perfection of the soul is in heaven, to see Christ face to face, and God in Christ. Heaven is the element of a Christian. It is his proper region. He is never well till there; and there is his rest, his solace and contentment, and there all his desires are satiated to the utmost. Till we be in heaven, we be under desires; for we be under imperfections. All the while we are in imperfections we are in an uncomfortable estate; and while we be so, we are not as we should be. And therefore wheresoever any are partakers of Christ's resurrection, they mind the ascension as present. Where any grace is, there the thoughts are for heaven presently.

Let us take a scanting[1] of our dispositions from hence. There be many that think it good to be here always; they never think of ascending. If they could live here always,

[1] That is, 'proportion' = measure. — G.

they would with all their hearts, but it is not so with a Christian. It is his desire to be where his happiness, his Saviour, his God and Father is, where his country and inheritance is, and therefore he mindeth ascension and things to come. When anything is done, he thinks that what is done is not yet enough. As your great conquerors in the world, they forget what they have conquered, and remember what they have yet to do; so Christ, having got conquest over death, he thinks now of ascension, to conquer in the eyes of all; for it is not enough to conquer in the field, but he will conquer in the city; he will conquer to heaven, and make show of his conquest. I ascend to lead captivity captive, 'to make a show', as it is expressed (Col. 2:15). While anything is to do or receive, our souls should not be satisfied, but still stretched out to desire further and further still, more and more still, till we be there where our souls shall be filled to the uttermost; and there is no place of further desire, as heaven is the place to satiate, and fill all the comers of the soul.

Quest. But how shall we know whether we be risen with Christ or no?

Resol. Partly we may know it by our former courses. Christ when he was risen, all the clothes were laid together in the grave. He left them behind, and rose with an earthquake. There was a commotion; and after his resurrection he minded heaven. So if ye be risen with Christ, your former vile courses lie in the grave; your oaths are gone; profaneness and wicked-ness of life gone. Tell you me, you are risen, while you carry the bonds of your sins about you? You profane, wretched, swearing, ungodly persons, filthy speakers, that have an heart more filthy, vile in body and soul, can they have any part in Christ? Where is that that bound you before? You carry it about still. Therefore you be in the bonds of the devil; you be in the grave of sin; there is no rising. Resurrection is with commotion. There was an earthquake when Christ arose; and there is an heartquake when the soul riseth. Can the soul rise from sin without commotion? In the inward man will there be division between flesh and spirit, without any ado at all? And therefore they that find nothing to do in their spirits, where is their rising again?

But that which is proper to the occasion in hand is the third. Where grace is begun, there will be an inward proceeding and ascending with Christ. How shall I know therefore whether I ascend?

1. First, *By minding things above*. The apostle telleth us directly (Col. 3:1), 'Mind things above', be heavenly-minded in some sort, live the life that Christ did, after his resurrection. All his discourse was, after his resur-rection, of the kingdom of heaven, and his mind was on the place whither he was to go; and so a true Christian indeed, that is truly risen, his thoughts and discourse is, when he is himself, heavenly. Other things he useth as if he did not; as while we be in the world, we must

deal with worldly things; but we must deal with them as that which is not our proper element (1 Cor. 7:31), 'They used the world, as if they used it not; and they married, as if they did not; for they knew the fashion of this world passeth away.' And therefore they that affect earthly glory, carnal affections and delights, they cannot think of these things with any comfort. They be moles which grovel in the earth. Some make a profession, and they ascend higher as kites do, but they look low; they make high professions, but their aims are low. The true eagles that ascend to Christ, as they ascend, so they look upward and upward still. They do not mind things below; they do not take a high pitch, and still continue earthly-minded; but they look high, as well as ascend high. Therefore let us not deceive ourselves.

2. Yet more particularly, those that ascend with Christ, they that are in heaven and they that are on earth *do the same things, though in different degrees and measure.* What do they in heaven? There they meddle not with defilements of the world; and so, though a Christian be on earth, he defileth himself not with the world, or ill company. He will converse with them, but not defile himself with them. They that be in heaven are praising God, and so be they much in praising of God here. They that be in heaven love to see the face of God, they joy in it. And they that be heavenly-minded here joy in the presence of God, in the word, the sacraments, and his children. If they be ascended

in any degree and measure, this they will do. And then they will joy in communion with God all they can, as they do in heaven. You have some carnal dispositions that are never themselves but in carnal company like themselves. If ever we mean to be in heaven, we must joy in heaven on earth; that is, in them that be heavenly in their dispositions. If we cannot endure them here, how shall we ever live with them in heaven?

The purpose of Christ's ascension

What was Christ to ascend for? What is the end of his ascension?

The end of his ascension was to take possession of heaven in his body, which had never been there before.

1. And he was to take possession of heaven in his body for his church; that is, his mystical body. So he ascended to heaven, carried his blessed body that he took in the virgin's womb with him.

2. And likewise he ascended to heaven, to take up heaven in behalf of his spouse, his church; as the husband takes up land in another country in behalf of his wife, therefore he did ascend.

3. And likewise he ascended to leave his Spirit, that he might send the Comforter. He taketh away himself, that was the great Comforter, while he was below. He was the bridegroom; and while the bridegroom was present, they had not such a measure of the Spirit. Christ's presence supplied all. But Christ ascended to heaven that his departure from them might not be prejudicial

to them, but that they might have comfort through the God of comfort, the Spirit of comfort, the Holy Ghost: 'I will send the Comforter' (John 14:16, *seq.*)

And though there was no loss by the ascension of Christ, they might fear by losing of Christ that all their comfort was gone. Ay, but Christ telleth them, 'I go to prepare a place for you.' He goeth to take up heaven for his church, and then to send his Spirit. What a blessed intercourse is there now, since Christ's ascension, between heaven and earth! Our body is in heaven, and the Spirit of God is here on earth. The flesh that he hath taken into heaven is a pledge that all our flesh and bodies shall be where he is ere long. In the mean time, we have the Spirit to comfort us, and never to leave us till we be brought to the place where Christ is. This is great comfort, and this is the main end why Christ ascended to the Father, that he might send the Comforter. And comfort might well come now in more abundance than before, because by the death of Christ all enemies were conquered, and by the resurrection of Christ it was discovered that God was appeased. The resurrection of Christ manifested to the world what was done by death; and now, all enemies being conquered, and God being appeased, what remains but the sweetest gift next to Christ, the Holy Ghost? And that is the reason why the Holy Ghost was more abundant after Christ's resurrection, because God was fully satisfied, and declared by the rising of Christ to be fully satisfied, and all enemies to be conquered.

4. One end likewise of his resurrection was 'to make a show of his conquest'. There is a double victory over the enemy. There is a victory in the field, and triumph together with it. And then there is triumphing *in civitate regia*, a triumphing in the kingly city. So Christ did conquer in his death, and showed his conquest by resurrection; but he did not lead captivity captive and make show thereof till he ascended; and then he made open show of his victorious triumph *in civitate regia*.

5. One special end, likewise, why he would have this message sent, that he was to ascend, was that he might appear there in heaven for us (as Heb. 7:25, 9:11, *seq.*), 'He appears for ever in heaven for us, and maketh intercession for us.' When the high priest was to enter into the holy of holies, which was a type of heaven, he carried the names of the twelve tribes engraven in stone upon his breast. Christ, our true high priest, being entered into the holy of holies, carried the names of all his elect in his breast into heaven, and there appeareth before God for us. He carrieth us in his heart. Christ doth fulfil that which in John 17 he prayeth for, appearing in heaven before his Father by virtue of his blood shed, and that blood that speaketh better things than the blood of Abel. It speaks mercy and pardon. The blood of Abel crieth for vengeance and justice; but the blood of Christ saith, Here is one that I shed my blood for. And when we pray to God, God accepts of our prayers; and by virtue of Christ's

blood shed, there is mercy, and pardon, and favour procured, which is sprinkled by faith upon the soul; God manifesting to the soul by his Spirit, that Christ died in particular for such a soul, which soul praying to God in the name of Christ, that blood not only in heaven, but sprinkled upon the soul, speaketh peace there. The Spirit saith that to the soul, which Christ doth in heaven. Christ saith in heaven, I died for such a soul; the Spirit saith in the soul, Christ died for me; and the blood of Christ is sprinkled on every particular soul. As Christ in heaven appears and intercedeth for me, so the Spirit intercedeth in mine own guilty heart, that always speaks discomfort, till it be satisfied with particular assurance. Christ died for me, and God is mine, and Christ is mine. Thus particular faith sprinkleth the blood of Christ upon the soul. So that now my sins are not only pardoned in heaven, but in my soul. There is not only intercession in heaven, but in my soul. My soul goeth to God for pardon and for mercy, and rejoiceth in all the mercies it hath and hopeth to have. What is done in heaven, is done in a man's soul by the Spirit in some measure.

6. The last end is, that he might show that our salvation is exactly wrought, that God is perfectly satisfied to the full, else he should never have risen, much less ascended to heaven. And therefore if we once believe in Christ for forgiveness of sins, and yet say, I doubt of salvation, it is all one as if you should go about to

pluck Christ from heaven. The doubtful, distrustful heart, till it be subdued by a spirit of faith, saith, 'Who shall ascend to heaven, to tell me whether I shall go to heaven?' or 'Who shall enter into the deep, to tell me I am freed from hell?' I am afraid I shall be damned, saith the guilty heart, till the Spirit of God hath brought it under and persuaded it of God's love in Christ. Say not, 'Who shall ascend up to heaven? for that is to bring Christ down from heaven' (Rom. 10:6, 7). And what an injurious thing is it to bring Christ down from heaven, to suffer on the cross! This is a great indignity, though we think not of it, to doubt of our salvation, and not cast ourselves on his mercy. For as verily as he is there, we shall be there. He is gone to take up a place for us. He is there in our name, as the husband taketh a place for his spouse. And if we doubt whether we shall come there or no, we doubt whether he be there or no. And if we doubt of that, we doubt whether he hath wrought salvation or no, and so we bring him down to the cross again. Who shall descend to the deep? that is, to bring Christ from the dead again. Such is the danger of a distrustful heart. So that by Christ's ascending into heaven, we may know all is done and accomplished; all our enemies are subdued; God is appeased and fully satisfied, heaven is taken up in our room, and therefore labour for a large heart answerable to the large unchangeable grounds we have, for faith to pitch and bottom itself upon it.

Christ pleading our cause

Therefore make this farther use of this ascension of Christ, and thereupon his intercession in heaven for us. He is there to plead our cause. He is there as our surety to appear for us, and not only so, but as a counsellor to plead for us; and not only so, but one of us, as if a brother should plead for a brother; and not only so, but a favourite there too. All favourites are not so excellent at counselling perhaps, but we have one that is favourite in heaven, and is excellent at pleading, that can non-suit all accusations laid against us by the devil. He is the Son of God, and he is one of us; he appeareth not as a stranger, for a stranger, as the counsellor is perhaps for his client, but he appears as our brother (Rev. 12:10). Let us think of the comforts of it. He appears for us to plead our cause, with acceptation of his person and cause. For he before whom he pleadeth, God the Father, sent him to take our nature, die, and ascend into heaven for us, to sustain the persons of particular offenders. He must needs hear Christ, that sent him for that purpose. Where the judge appoints a counsel, it is a sign he favoureth the cause. Perhaps we cannot pray, are disconsolate, and vexed with Satan's temptations. The poor client hath a good cause, but cannot make a good cause of it. But if he get a skilful lawyer, that is favourable to him, and before a favourable judge, his comfort is, his advocate can make his cause good. If we would confess our sins, as that we must do, we must take shame to ourselves in all our distress and

73

disconsolation of spirit; and we must lay open our estates to God, and complain; and then desire God to look upon us, and Christ to plead our cause for us and answer Satan; and when Satan is very malicious and subtle, as he is a very cunning enemy to allege all advantages against us, to make us despair, remember this, we have one in heaven that is more skilful than he 'that is the accuser of brethren' (Rev. 12:10), that accuseth us to God and to our own souls, that accuseth every man to himself and maketh him an enemy to himself. But we have a pleader in heaven that will take our part against the accuser of our brethren, and quiet us at length in our consciences. Perhaps we may be troubled a while, to humble us; but remember that he is in heaven purposely to plead our cause.

It is a good plea to God, 'Lord, I know not what to say; my sins are more than the hairs of my head. Satan layeth hard to me. I cannot answer one of a thousand. I confess all my sins. Hear me, and hear thy Son for my sake. He is now at thy right hand, and pleadeth for me.' And desire Christ to plead for us. We have not only all the church to pray for us, 'Our Father'; but we have Christ himself to plead for us and make our cause good, if Christ saith, I shed my blood for this person, and [he] appears now by virtue of my redemption. And the condition of the covenant is, if we confess our sins, he is merciful to forgive. And if we sin, we have an advocate in heaven, to whom we must lay claim (1 John 2:1). The party hath confessed the debt; and therefore the bond must be cancelled. He hath performed the conditions on his part; and therefore make it good on thine own part. And seeing the Spirit hath shamed thee for thy sins, what can the devil say? What saith Paul? 'It is God that justifieth; who shall condemn?' (Rom. 8:33). If God, the party offended, do justify, who shall condemn? It is Christ that died. That is not enough. 'That is risen again.' That is not enough. It is Christ that rose again, 'and sitteth at the right hand of God for us', and maketh intercession for us. 'Who shall lay any thing to the charge of God's elect?' Let the devil accuse what he will, Christ is risen, to show that he hath satisfied; and is now in heaven, there appearing for us. Oh that we had hearts large enough for these comforts! then should we never yield to base temptations.

The comfort of an ascended Christ
It is against the pleasure of God that we should be disconsolate. Therefore we wrong our own souls, and sin against our own comfort, when we let the reins loose by inordinate and extreme sorrow. We lose that sweetness that we might enjoy, by giving way to discomfortable thoughts. Indeed, if a man examine his life from the beginning of his conversion to the end thereof, he may thank himself for all his trouble. The sin against the holy gospel is a kind of rebellion against God, though we think not so, when we will not be comforted, nor embrace grounds of comfort when we have them. The comforts of God ought not

to be of small esteem to us. The sweet comforts, large, exceeding, eternal comforts of God, we ought to esteem of them as they be; and therefore our Saviour Christ sendeth to them speedily.

All Scripture is to this end, for consolation, even the Scripture that tendeth to instruction and direction, that so men may be in a state of comfort; for cordials are not good, but where there is purgation before. So all Scriptures that are purging, to tell us our faults, they be to bring us unto a comfortable condition. Other Scriptures, that tend to instruct our judgments and settle us in faith, what is the end of all, if we walk not comfortably towards God and strongly in our places? Therefore, when we look not to comfort and joy in all conditions, we abuse the intendments[1] of God.

But, I beseech you, make not a bad use of it; for if you know it to be so, if it worketh not graciously in you, and winneth you to respect God the more, and love him that is thus indulgent and gracious, but go on in offending conscience, and break peace off, then at length conscience will admit no comfort. Many that have excellent comforts have made havoc of their consciences, and will go on in spite of ministers, in spite of their consciences and God's Spirit joined with conscience. At length it is just with God to give them up to despair, wicked sinners that trample the blood of Christ under their feet. But for all other that strive

---

[1] That is, 'intentions.' — G.

against corruption, and would be better, it is a ground of marvellous comfort.

I shall come to the message itself. Tell them, 'I ascend.' He speaketh of that as present which was surely to be. So we should think of our future estate as if we were presently to go to heaven. Faith hath this force, to make things to come present. If we could keep it in us, and exercise it, could we live in any sin? But that it is distant, that is the cause of sinning. We put off things in a distance. If it be at the day of judgment, that is far off; and therefore they will not leave their present pleasure for that that shall not be, they know not when. But look on things in the word of a God that is Jehovah, that giveth a being to all, who hath spoken of things to come as if present, and then you will be of another mind. Faith is the privilege of a Christian, which maketh things afar off present. No wicked man but would leave his swearing and profaneness if he saw the joys of heaven and pains of hell; and it were no thanks to him. But to believe God on his word, that these things shall be, that is the commendations of a man, and the excellency of a Christian above another man. Another man doth all by sense; but the Christian will trust God on his word. 'I ascend', saith Christ.

We must not think of the ascension of Christ as a severed thing from us, but if we would have the comfort of it, we must think of it as ourselves ascending with him. Think of Christ as a public person and surety for us, and then we shall have great comfort in that, that he saith, 'I ascend'. God prepared paradise before he made the creature. He would have him to come into a place of honour and pleasure. And so God, before ever we were born, provided a place and paradise for us in heaven, that we might end our days with greater comfort. We may be straitened here. Many a good Christian hath scarce where to lay his head; but Christ is gone to prepare a place for them in heaven. And this may comfort us in the consideration of all our sins; for sin past, and for corruption present, and sin that we may commit for time to come. For anything that is past, if we confess our sins to God, he will forgive them. 'The blood of Christ cleanseth us from all sins' (1 John 1:7), even from the present corruptions that attend on us. We have one that stands between God and us as a surety; and he will give us his Spirit to subdue our corruptions, and at length make us like himself, a glorious spouse (Eph. 5:27). If we were perfect men, we need not a mediator; and this may teach us comfort, rather because we are sinners, and daily subject to offend God. We have one to make our peace for time to come; if we sin, we have an advocate (1 John 2:1). When Christ taught us to pray, 'Forgive us our daily trespasses', he supposed we should run daily into sins (Matt. 6:12). We have an advocate in heaven every day to stand between God and us, to answer God, to undertake that at length we should cease to offend him; and for the present, we are such as he shed his precious blood for; and he appeareth for us by virtue of his death, which is a marvellous comfort. We think if we commit sin there is no hope. But what needs a mediator, but to make peace between the parties disagreeing? If all things were made up between God and us, what need of an intercessor? But God knoweth well enough we run into daily sins, by reason of a spring of corruption in us, which is never idle. And therefore we may daily go to God in the name of our advocate, and desire God for Christ's sake to pardon, and desire Christ to intercede for us. Let us therefore shame ourselves.

There is not a Christian but will be in himself apprehensive of being thrown into hell every day. There is a spring of corruption in him, and should God take a forfeiture of[1] his daily rebellions, his conscience tells him it were just. And therefore we must every day live upon this branch of his priestly office, his mediation. We must live by faith in this branch of Christ, and make use of it continually, for this will keep us from hell. And therefore if we sin every day, go to God in the name of Christ, and desire him to pardon us. This is to feed on Christ; and therefore we should more willingly come to the sacrament. When we be in heaven, we shall need a mediator no longer, for we shall be perfectly holy. We cannot think of these things too much. They be the life of religion and of comforts; and it may teach us to make a true use of Christ in all our conditions. Poor souls that are not acquainted

[1] That is, 'from' = should God regard his rebellion as a 'forfeiture', *etc.*—G.

with the gospel, they think God will cast them into hell for every sin, and they live as if they had not an high priest in heaven to appear for them.

Christ's Father and ours

The matter of the message is, Christ ascended to God, as a common Father and God to him and them. He doth not say, I ascend to the Father. That were no great comfort; for what were that to them? or to my Father only. Neither doth he say, 'I ascend to our Father', for that is true in the order of it: for he is not in equal respect the God and Father of Christ, and the God and Father of us. And therefore he speaks of himself in the first place: 'I go to my God and your God.' For he is first and specially Christ's Father and Christ's God, and then ours; as we shall see in the particulars. We have a common Father and a common God with Christ. God the Father is Christ's Father by eternal generation, as he is God and man. We have therefore the nature of Christ as he is God and man.

There is this difference between God's being Christ's Father and the Father of any else.

First of all, God is Christ's Father from eternity. God had a being and was a Father from all eternity. There is no man of equal standing with his father. He is born after his father cometh to be a man. But Christ is of God from all eternity. His generation is eternal; and therefore there is a grand difference.

Then Christ is co-equal with the Father in glory and

majesty every day. The son is not equal with the father, but Christ is with his Father.

Again, The son in other generations comes of the father, and is like the father, taken out of his substance, but of a different substance from the father. But Christ and the Father, both the persons are in one substance, in one essence. The essence of the Father differeth not from the essence of the Son. We must remember this, to give Christ the prerogative and pre-eminency, that God is his Father in another manner than ours. He is his Father by nature, ours by adoption. What he is by nature, we are by grace. Though Christ was intent upon his ascension, yet he forgetteth not this grand difference here, but mentioneth it: 'Go to my brethren.' We must not call him brother again. We may think of him as our brother; but 'My God and my Lord', as Thomas saith (John 20:28). If the greatest person should call us brother, yet it is most behoveful for the inferior to say, 'My God, my Lord'; to acknowledge Christ as a great person, and to make use of his love to strengthen our faith, not to diminish our respect to him in any way. It is his infinite mercy to term us brethren. But when we go to him we must have other terms.

Thus we see how to conceive of Christ after his resurrection. When he hath triumphed over all his enemies, and reconciled God by his death, then 'I go to my Father and your Father'. Then he is a common Father, by virtue of Christ's satisfaction to divine wrath and justice, and victory and triumphing over all his enemies. So we must not conceive of God as our Father, but in reference to Christ's victory over death. God is our Father by virtue of Christ's satisfaction to justice and conquest over all our enemies. 'The God of peace', saith the holy apostle Paul in the epistle to the Hebrews, in the conclusion of that excellent epistle, 'that brought you from death to life through our Lord Jesus Christ' (John 5:24). How cometh he to be the God of peace to us, which brought us from death to life by our Lord Jesus? Why, the resurrection of Christ makes him the God of peace. Who raised him? He raised himself. But who together with himself? The Father raised him. And could the Father raise him if he were not reconciled? But now he is the 'God of peace'; for peace is made by the cross and blood of Christ (Col. 3:15), the great peace-maker of heaven and earth; now we may conceive of God under the sweet relation of a Father.

Now this relation of a father teacheth us as what we may expect from God, so what we ought to return to God again, and how we ought to carry ourselves one towards another.

I. *What we may expect from God being a Father.*

(1.) *We may expect whatsoever a child may expect from a father*. God taketh not upon him empty names. He saith he will be a Father, not only called a Father, 'but I will be your Father, and you shall be my sons' (2 Cor. 6:18). All the fatherhood, and all the kindred in heaven and earth that is spiritual, the comfort of it cometh from God the Father, reconciled to us in Christ. The word in the original is so strong that we cannot express it in English. Fathers on earth are but poor fathers, and they be but beams of the fatherly affection that is in God. God will let us see by these beams of compassion that is in a father to a child, what real compassion he beareth to us. The true reality of fatherhood is in God. And therefore, when we hear of father, think of whatsoever lieth in the bowels of a father to a child; and that we may expect from God our Father, and infinite more. It is a great indulgence; as a father pitieth his child, so God will pity us (Mal. 3:17). Will a father cast off his child,? Indeed, he will cleanse the child. So God will take away our abominations, and purge us when we defile ourselves. It is because of an eternal relation he casteth us not off. We may expect from him indulgence; and it is an indulgence of indulgence. God needed no son when he made us sons. Yet he had his Son and angels to praise himself withal. Can we pity and pardon a child? and will not God pardon and pity us? Why should we conceive worse of him than of ourselves? Will we give pity to a father, and not pity to the Father of all bowels and compassion? And therefore think not that God will cast us off. God pardons us, and healeth our infirmities, and pitieth us as a father pitieth his own child (Psa. 103:13). It is a name under which no man must despair. What! Despair under the name of a father? Despair of mercy when we have a Father to go to?

The poor prodigal, when he had spent his patrimony, his body, his good name, had lost all, and nothing left, yet he had a father, and 'I will go to him' (Luke 15:18). And so, when we be at the last cast, and have spent all, we have a Father. Therefore go to him. What saith the church? (Isa. 63, 64), 'Doubtless thou art our Father', when the church was in a poor condition; 'Though our righteousness be as a menstruous cloth, and we be defiled, yet thou art our Father; we are the clay, thou art the potter,' *etc.* So that it is a name of his indulgence.

You have his disposition set down by the father of the prodigal. The son saith, he will *go* to the father; the father *runneth* to him and meeteth him when he is coming. God runneth to us, and is ready to meet us, when we begin to repent of sin, and are sensible of our faults. He is more ready to pardon, than we to ask pardon.

I touch only some principal things, that you may remember against the evil day and hour of temptation. He taketh not on him the relation of a Father for nought, but will fill it up to the uttermost. It is no empty relation.

(2.) *It is a name likewise of comfort.* It is the speech of a natural man, 'A little punishment is enough from a father.' 'He knoweth whereof we are made, he remembers we are but dust' (Psa. 103:14, and Heb. 12:6); he knoweth we are not iron or steel; he knoweth our making; and therefore he will deal gently with us when he doth correct us. It is as necessary as our daily bread to have gentle correction, to wean us from the world; yet he doth it gently. A little punishment will serve from a gracious father.

(3.) *It is a name likewise of provision*, that we may expect from God; that he will in all our exigences and necessities provide for us whatsoever shall be needful. What saith our Saviour Christ to the poor disciples doubting of want? 'It is your Father's good will to give you the kingdom.' What then? 'Fear not, little flock' (Luke 12:32). He that will give you a kingdom, will not he give you daily bread, *viaticum*, provision for a journey? He that intendeth us heaven, certainly he will provide for us here. And therefore in the Lord's prayer, before all petitions, as a ground of all, he putteth in 'our Father'; and therefore, 'Give us our daily bread, our Father.' And therefore he will give us grace to sanctify his name, and do his will, and forgive us our sins. Expect all from our Father, which is the ground of all. Christ had much ado to persuade his disciples that they should not want necessaries; and therefore he makes whole sermons to strengthen their faith in this: 'Your heavenly Father knoweth what you stand in need of' (Matt. 6:8). The son cannot ask, but the Father can interpret any sigh, any groan, and knoweth what we would have. And therefore being God's children, we may fetch provision from him in all conditions.

(4.) *And with provisions, protection likewise*; and therefore make this use of it. In the temptations of Satan, lie under the wing of our Father. We have a Father to go to; make use of him, make use of his protection, that God would shield us, that he would be a tower, as he is a tower, and 'the righteous man may fly to him' (Prov. 18:10). Lie under his wings. He is a gracious Father, and he hath taken this sweet relation on him for this purpose, that we may have comfort in all conditions. You see then what we may expect from God, by this sweet relation he hath taken on him in Christ, to be our Father.

II. *This word, it is a word of relation.*

It bindeth God to us and us to God. We are to honour him as our Father. This one word is sufficient to express our duty to a father, and that is a word of reverence; for it includeth a mixed affection of fear and love. And it is an affection of an inferior to a superior. He is great, therefore we ought to fear him. He is good, therefore we ought to love him. There is with him beams of majesty and bowels of compassion. As there is beams of majesty, we ought to fear him; as bowels of compassion, we ought to love him. So that fear and love mixed together is the affection we owe to God as our Father. If we tremble, and are afraid to go to him, we know not he is loving. If we go to him over-boldly and saucily, we forget that he is great. Therefore we must think of his greatness, that we forget not his goodness. We must so think of his goodness, that we forget not his greatness. Therefore go boldly to him, with reverence to the throne of Christ. In the word 'Father', there is more saving power than in ten thousand. It toucheth his very bowels. When a child wanteth anything, and is in distress, let it but say, Father, or Mother, and the parents yearn upon him. If God be our Father, go to him boldly; but with reverence go with affiance[1] to his bowels. Oh, it is a persuasive word! What cannot we look from[2] that majesty that hath condescended to be called 'Father', and to be a Father to us in all our necessities? Either we shall have what we want and lack, or else we shall have that which is better. He is a wise Father. He answereth not always according to our wills, but always according to our good. He seeth it is for our good that we are not presently comforted. The physician giveth a sharp potion. Oh, I cannot endure! And the surgeon lanceth. Oh, I cannot endure it! But the surgeon knoweth it is not healing time. Even so we would be presently taken off from under crosses; but God is a wise Father, and knoweth how long it is fit for us to continue under the cross.

Come to him boldly therefore, under the name of a father, that he may move his bowels, and surely will hear us. For in Psalm 27:10, when all forsook me, 'My father and mother forsook me, but the Lord took me up.' Fathers in the flesh, and mothers, die, but the Lord

[1] That is, 'trust'.—G.
[2] Qu. 'look for him'?—Ed.

taketh us up. He is an eternal Father, and therefore a ground of eternal boldness with God, and of everlasting comfort. He was our Father before we had a father in the world, and he will be our Father when we shall cease to be in the world. They be but instruments under God to bring us into the world. God is our true Father. Our other fathers are but under God, to give us a being, to fit us for heaven. He provideth the best inheritance and paternity for us in heaven. And therefore never be disconsolate, but remember, 'I go to my Father and your Father,' which is a word of eternal comfort. He was our Father from eternity in election; he will be our Father to eternity in glorification. 'Can a mother forget her child? yea, though she should, yet can I not forget thee, thou art written in the palm of my hand' (Isa. 49:15, 16). God hath us always in his eye. A mother cannot always think of her child. She sleepeth sometimes; but God is a Father that never sleepeth. 'The keeper of Israel neither slumbereth nor sleepeth' (Psa. 121:4). And this is our comfort in all times and for eternity. And therefore we ought to carry ourselves to God reverently, and go boldly to him, and always make use of him.

And this we should learn likewise, to maintain a sweet frame between God and us. Shall God open such an advantage to us? Shall God be our Father, and bear the gracious eternal affection of a father? and shall not we, by prayer and faith, fetch from our Father all we stand in need of? As our Saviour saith, 'You that be earthly fathers, when your children ask such a thing, will you deny?' (Matt. 7:9, 10). And have we a Father so rich, so loving, and shall not we have intercourse with him in our daily necessities? What a trade is open to us, if we know what a comfort is laid up in the sweet relation of a father! 'Your Father knoweth what we stand in need of' (Matt. 6:8), and he will give thee the spring of all graces, not only a broken heart, a spirit of life and vigour in his service, but go to God and he will give thee his Holy Spirit, which is the best thing next Christ that can be. And therefore be encouraged to make intercourse between thee and God, considering we have a brother in heaven, our nature is there, and our spirit is below. We have the best things in heaven, next Christ, on earth, and God hath our flesh in heaven by Christ; and therefore why should we not be much in prayer, and much in praises in all our necessities? Beloved, it is a comfort of that largeness that I cannot express it. I rather leave it to your admiration, that you may see what use to make of this sweet relation of a father.

(1.) But we must know, that every one cannot say, 'my Father', for there are a company of men in the world that may say, in some respects, 'our Father'; but in other respects they cannot. As our Saviour Christ saith peremptorily (John 8:44), 'You are of your father the devil.' They bragged of God their Father, and they were of their 'father the devil'. Therefore, consider who is fit to take this name into their mouths, 'My Father'. Mark the disposition of the scribes and Pharisees, and then you shall see who be fit to brag of God as their Father. They be very formal men, look to their outward devotion, who so devout as they? They studied it; but what were they for the inside? They were malicious men, they were satanical men, men opposite to the power of religion, arrant hypocrites, painted sepulchres. It is no matter for compliment or formality. An hypocrite may have much of that in the eyes of the world, yet may be a child of the devil for all that, and a Pharisee for all that. Thou mayest be malicious against the truth, as the Pharisees sought Christ's blood. A man may be like Herod, seeking the blood of Christ in his members, persecuting Christ, as all cruel men do. They seek to devour Christ in his professors. What they can, they disparage and dishearten them. They are enemies to the power of religion and to the ordinances of God. They be the children of the devil, and therefore have no reason at all to brag that God is their Father. Indeed, an inward bitter disposition against the power of religion, though under any formality, is a character of a satanical spirit, and such cannot say, 'Our Father'. If they do, it is an usurpation, for their true father is the devil.

(2.) *Who can say, Our Father?* Those that by the Spirit of the Father and the Son, by the Holy Ghost, are ingrafted into Christ by a spirit of adoption, and have the stamp of the Father upon them. The likeness of the Father and of Christ, whom God begets to his own likeness, that are, in a word, like Christ. Christ is the first Son, and in him, and for his sake, we are sons. He is the natural Son, and they may say 'Our Father' that labour to express the disposition of Christ, who is the first Son. See this disposition of Christ in the gospel, how marvellously patient he was under the hand of his Father, obedient to the death of his cross, humbled, full of love, full of goodness. 'He went about doing good' (Acts 10:38). Do we then walk as Christ did? Carry we the image of the 'second Adam'? Have we the patient, humble, meek disposition of Christ in our measure? Do we love Christ in his members, God in his image? Do we love the ordinances and the power of religion? This showeth what we are. And is our conversation suitable to our inward disposition? Do we walk in light? Do we show by our conversation whose children we are? Do our speeches give a character of the inward man? If this be in us, though in never so small a measure, with comfort we may say, 'Our Father.'

But may not another man, that is not in Christ, come to God under the sweet name of 'our Father'? Yea, he may come to him as his father by creation and providence, or sacramentally a father, or as brought into the church, and having God to create him and to provide for him. Lord, thou hast showed thyself a gracious Father thus far, though I cannot from any inward persuasion say, 'My Father.' Thus far as I can I say, 'My Father.' Strive against our spiritual infidelity, believe God and cast ourselves on his gracious promises in Christ. God will meet us at the same time, and he will send us his

Spirit to make us his sons. And therefore let no man that hath been a wicked liver be discouraged from going to God in the name of a father, in that wherein he is a father. Lord, thou hast created me and preserved me, and it is thy mercy I am not in hell. Yet thou offerest to be my Father in Christ – thou hast made gracious promises and invited me; and upon this, when the heart yieldeth to the gracious apprehensions of God as a Father, there is a spirit of faith wrought in the heart presently. Therefore think of the name of a father, and the very thoughts of it will bring the spirit of adoption.

Only it speaks no comfort to the bitter, malicious, satanical enemies of Christ, and the power of religion. They be children of the devil. But now poor souls, that groan under the burden of sin, let them think that God is a Father, and of the mercies of God, though they do not see they be interested in them. By the very contemplation of the mercies of God in Christ, and his inviting them to receive them, the Spirit of God will be wrought in the soul, whereby they may have confidence to come to God as a Father.

The comfort of having God as our Father
I desire you therefore to remember this. It is the first sermon of our Saviour Christ after his resurrection, and therefore forget not to think of God as a Father and Christ as a Brother. Indeed, whatsoever comfort is in any relation, God and Christ have taken it on them. A father is more comprehensive than any other title: Christ

is Father, and Husband, and Spouse. And God is our Rock and Shield; and whatsoever is comfortable he hath taken on him, and in Christ we may command him to be so. And if we had ten thousand worlds, they could not be compared to the comforts that arise from hence, that we can call God, Father. It is more to us, if we could improve it in our spiritual trade for heaven, than if we had a thousand worlds, especially in days of affliction and in the hour of death. For it improveth whatsoever is in the bowels of God for poor, distressed souls. When nothing else will comfort, this will comfort, if we can say to God, 'Father'. Though we cannot make a distinct prayer, yet if we can say 'Father', God can pick matter out of our broken language. Now Christ is ascended up to heaven, he doth us more good than he did when he was upon the earth. The sun in the firmament yieldeth us heat and comfort; but if it were nearer it would do us hurt, or if further off it would not do us so much good. God hath placed it, being a common light of the world, high, to enlighten inferior bodies, and to convey influence by means into them. And so Christ, the Sun of righteousness, being ascended and advanced to heaven, doth more good than on earth. And therefore saith he, 'It is for your good that I ascend.' It is for our good that we have Christ in heaven, to appear there for us.

'I ascend to my Father, and to your Father.' 'Father' is here taken personally, not essentially; though it be true in that sense, 'to my Father', as the first person of the Trinity especially. Christ may well say, 'I ascend to my

Father' now; for he was risen again, and was mightily declared to be the Son of God by his resurrection from the dead. 'Thou art my Son; this day I have begotten thee'; that is, this day have I declared thee (Rom. 1:4, and Heb. 1:5). It is said of things, *fiunt, cum patefiunt*, they are done when they be open, and declared to be done. Christ was the Son of God when he rose again, because he was discovered by his glorious resurrection to be so indeed. And therefore Christ may well say after his resurrection, 'I go to my Father, and your Father.' Observe from hence, that God in Christ is our Father. We say, relations are *minimæ entitates*, they are little entities founded upon others, but they are *maximæ consequents*, of great concernment.

God's love in Christ

I beseech you, before I leave the point, give me leave to go on a little further in this, to show that wonderful mercy, that admirable goodness which the tongues and hearts of all the men in the world, and angels in heaven, are not able to express; that love of God which is contained in the relation he hath taken on him in Christ to be our Father.

(1.) *Consider who, and whom*. Who, the great God, that hath the Son to solace himself in. He did not adopt us because he wanted sons. He had sons of his own, and sons of his love to solace himself in. What need he have took traitors, rebels, enemies, to make them his sons? Oh it is a marvellous advancement of our

94

nature, that God should in Christ become our 'Father'. It is said (Psa. 113:6), 'God abaseth himself to behold things below'; and indeed so he doth, with reverence be it spoken to his great majesty: he abaseth himself in regard of things below, in regard of us worms of the earth, that be enemies, yea, devils by nature. For many, ye shall see the devil in them, in their lying and opposing of goodness. And God will always have some amongst men, to show others what they would be, if God left them to themselves. God abaseth himself to behold things below. Not that it is a diminution of majesty to do it, but God in Christ hath stooped so low, that he could go no lower, and he is advanced as high in our nature as can be. How could God become a man, a curse, God in the second person with us, God in the first person to be so near to us as a Father, and God in the second person to make him a Father, to be so low as Christ was, which is to be as low as hell itself?

(2.) *Consider to whom this message is sent.* He is your Father, even a Father to you the disciples, now you are disconsolate. God owneth us for his children at the worst. He took our condition notwithstanding all our infirmities. When we be pronest by a work of the Spirit to condemn ourselves, then God is nearest to justify us. When the poor prodigal said, 'I am unworthy to be a son, make me an household servant', you see how the father entertaineth him (Luke 15:19). So the poor publican dareth not lift up his eyes, and yet went away justified (Luke 18:13). David, when he could not pray, but murmur and rebel, and said in his heart all men are liars, 'yet thou heardest the voice of my prayer' (Psa. 116:11); even then, when he could not pray, but groan and sigh to God: 'I said, I am cast out of thy sight, yet thou regardest the voice of my prayers'; when he said, out of a murmuring spirit and rebelliousness of nature, I am cast out of thy sight – a speech that tended to desperation, – yet God heard the voice of his prayer. When Job said, 'I clothed myself in dust and ashes', God said to him, 'I have accepted thee' (Job 42:6, 8). When we by the Spirit think ourselves unworthy to be accepted, or to look to heaven, or to tread upon the earth, then God looketh on us worthy in his Son; and never more worthy than when we acknowledge our own unworthiness. 'Go tell my disciples', at this time when they had dealt so unworthily, 'I go to their Father'.

It is from his own bowels, and not any goodness in us, that he loveth us. He loveth the work of his own Spirit, his own nature, that that is of his own. Though the child hath many infirmities, yet the Father seeth the nature of the child, and therefore loveth it. God seeth his image of holiness in us in some poor measure, and he loveth his own in us. And he loveth our love to him, which is in some measure. Though the disciples had got into corners, after their unkind dealing with Christ, yet he knew they loved him. As where there is love, there will be a reflection of his love back again.

And then God knoweth if he should not show mercy to sinners, he should have none to serve him on earth. And therefore saith the psalmist (Psa. 130:4), 'There is mercy with thee that thou mayest be feared'; that is, worshipped. If God were not merciful to sinners, where should he have any to worship him? And therefore God showeth himself to be a Father, even to sinful creatures; even in their wickedness, he seeth his own nature in them. He seeth some love, some work of respect in them, and if he should not love them, he would have none to fear him.

Beloved, live upon this. I spake before of the love of Christ. Here is the love of God the Father, who is content to be a Father even in our sinful condition. If God be a Father to us, as to Christ, then let not our hearts be discouraged in afflictions, persecutions, temptations. God was a Father to Christ in his desertion. God leaveth us to ourselves sometimes, and we fear his love. Did not he leave his own Son upon the cross – 'My God, my God, why hast thou forsaken me?' (Matt. 27:46) – and yet he ceased not to be a Father.

For persecution of enemies: was not Christ's whole life filled up with persecution, and yet a Son? For temptations: thou art tempted, and thinkest thou art none of God's children. Satan did tempt our blessed Saviour, that he might be a merciful Saviour, and know how to succour thee in times of temptation. Therefore, be not discouraged. Say not, when thou art deserted, persecuted, afflicted, tempted, God is not thy Father;

for by that reason thou mayest argue, God was none of Christ's Father. God was Christ's Father, notwithstanding his desertion for a time; and notwithstanding his afflictions in the world, his persecutions of all sorts of men, and notwithstanding his temptations, God was his Father still. This we must observe, 'father' is not a relation today, none tomorrow. It is an eternal relation. *'Dum percutis, pater es; dum castigas, pater es'*, saith Augustine:[1] 'While thou strikest us, thou art our Father; whilst thou correctest us, thou art our Father.' Parents are tender to their weakest and sick children; and God is most tender of all to them that be weak. 'Go, tell Peter.' And therefore, never be out of conceit of God or Christ. We cannot be in a condition wherein, on any sound grounds, we may run from God.

Be indulgent in preaching the truth

But if this be so, let us learn of God to be indulgent. If I were to speak to ministers, I should be large to advise them to preach the law and the gospel. The very law is preached in mercy. The Lord taketh a severe course, but it is to order us. All God's severity is reducible to mercy and Christ; all his afflictions, humiliations, and abasements, do they come from unfatherly affection? No; but to draw us home to him. And therefore, never be terrible to any, but with a bowel of compassion, but with a mind that they may see themselves, and see the

---

[1] One of the often-recurring apophthegms of the *Confessions* and theology of this Father.—G.

comforts they have in Christ. We ought to be of his affection, the great Pastor and Bishop of the church. And so for ordinary Christians; they should be indulgent one to another. Some are always cutting in ulcers; always wounding and tearing themselves with ill usage and misconstruction; keeping themselves from growing up in a better life, by observing the infirmities of them that be better than themselves. Oh, but 'go, tell my brethren' that my Father owneth them for his children, which may be a use of marvellous comfort to us.

Shall a child be always prowling for itself? We think there is neither father nor mother to take care for it: your heavenly Father knoweth what you need. We ought to labour for contentment in all conditions; for God is our Father. And for others, if God be our Father, let us look to others that be our brethren; own them, and carry ourselves to them as brethren. Let the strong carry themselves lowly to the weak. It is a sign of greatest strength to be most indulgent. Many account it great commendations on their part to be censorious and to be severe. Ay, but that is the greatest part of their weakness, if they have any goodness in them. For who was more indulgent to the disciples than Christ, who saw their weakness? He bore with all their infirmities. Where we see any goodness, let us bear with many weaknesses. We ought to be peaceable men: *Beati sunt pacifici.*[1] They that be appeased in their consciences, in sense of their

---

[1] That is, 'Blessed are the peace-makers.' Cf. Matt. 5:9.—G.

own pardon, are ready to show mercy to others. Busy, contentious, quarrelsome dispositions argue they never found comfort from God himself.

If God be a Father, and we are brethren, it is a levelling word; it bringeth mountains down and filleth up valleys. All are brethren, take them in what condition you will. If they be great in the world, brethren of high degree; yet 'brother' levelleth them. If they be of low degree, yet it filleth them up, and raiseth them to the height in this brotherhood. And therefore, 'Go, tell my brethren'; tell them all, for they be all equally brethren.

If I were to speak to persons of quality and great parts, as I am to speak to mean, let them be put in mind of their condition. Nothing should raise us up so high, as to forget the everlasting relation of brother. Infirmity should not so far prevail with us, as to forget that which the children of God have to eternity. And for other persons more eminent, if he be a king, let him not so mind that, as to forget all other. For all relations determine in death, and must be laid in the dust; all must stand on equal ground before God's bar, and they that have most to answer for, have the highest account of all, and therefore it is ground of humility to all. Let them that are in greatest eminency consider this. Paul, after conversion, could say, 'Henceforth, I know no man after the flesh' (2 Cor. 5:16). There is a great deal of humanity in the world: compliment is very ordinary, which is the picture and outside of humanity; but Christian love, which is a degree above humanity, the apostle calleth it φιλαδελφια [*philadelphia*], 'brotherly love', that is the scorn of the world. They will own a brother in office; but owning them in the sweet bonds of brotherhood, as they are the sons of God, here is heaven; make much of them in that kind, that is a strange thing in the world. But we must know what it meaneth, before we come to heaven. We must respect a Christian, be he what he will be, under all his infirmities, if he hath a good spirit in him, which God the Father seeth and Christ seeth. We must bear love to all saints. Some will make much of an eminent man, that hath excellent parts, because there may be some countenance from such persons; but here is sincerity that beareth love to all saints. He wraps them up all in the general term, 'Go, tell Peter', among the rest, that hath offended more than the rest.

Knowing true brethren
If you will know whether you be true brethren or no, or sons of God or no, make a use of trial, by what is formerly delivered. I shall enlarge myself in that point, because all dependeth upon it. God is the Father of all by creation; he is the Father in a general covenant, of all that receive the sacrament and are baptised. But if they have no other relation to God but so, they may go to hell, as Judas and others did: therefore we must know whether we may claim this relation of Father on good grounds or no, else it is an usurpation.

1. Those that belong to God, *the Spirit of God witnesseth to them that they are sons*. They that are

adopted have the Spirit of adoption in some degree. God sendeth his Spirit into their hearts, that assures them that they be God's children. And howsoever this is the first, yet God giveth some intimation by his Spirit, that they look to God in another familiar manner than before; and he looks on them in a fatherly manner. So there be some intimations, and insinuations, and hints, though the Spirit of adoption witnesseth not fully and gloriously to the soul always, because we are not fitted for it; but sometimes in great afflictions and desertions. Where the Spirit of God is, there is communion with God in the Spirit of adoption. And when the voice of the Spirit of adoption speaks not loudly, yet there is a work of the Spirit. There is something to us renewed by the Spirit; there is something of the new creature. When a Christian cannot hear God say to his soul, 'I am thy salvation', yet a man may see a work of grace. There is a love to God, to the ordinances, to the people of God; a mourning, because he cannot mourn; a sighing, because he hath not an heart pliable. He is discordant with his condition when he is disconsolate. So that there is a work of the Spirit helpeth him in his worst condition.

Besides, there is a spirit of supplication in some measure. Though he cannot make set discourses to God, yet he can in a sweet manner lay open his sorrow and grief to God, and leave them in his bosom. They be broken words, perhaps, but God can pluck sense out of them. God knoweth the meaning of the sighing of his own Spirit, though broken speeches. So that where there is any tongue for God in a man, there is a spirit of prayer; there is not a strangeness of God to go altogether by, but the spirit hath a kind of acquaintance with God; and it goeth to God in a familiarity, and layeth forth grief, and putteth forth petitions, in another manner than the world doth.

Again, a Christian in the worst condition, God not only shineth on him through the cloud, but there is a spirit in him that sigheth to go through all thick clouds to God. There is a spirit of supplication and of love in some degree, for that is promised. 'The Spirit shall help our infirmities, when we know not how to pray' (Rom. 8:26). The intercourse and communion with God is never broken off where there is any Spirit of adoption. Therefore Jonah and David, and the rest, though they could not pray, yet they sighed to God, and would not leave him. If they could embrace Christ, they would not leave him. If they could not embrace Christ, they would touch the hem of his garment. They will not yield to the stream altogether, but strive against it. And though they be carried away with the strength of the stream, and see no goodness in themselves, yet they that be with them shall see a spirit striving to another condition than they are in. Something of Christ's, something of God's Spirit there will be in them. And take them at the worst, they will appear better than the civil man, that thinks himself a glorious man, though he hath nothing but for show and fashion. Who would be in such a man's condition without some brokenness of heart, some sighs?

2. Likewise we may know it *by our sympathy and antipathy* – our sympathy with them that be good, and antipathy to that which is naught.[1] There is a love of that which is good. So things, good things, are connatural to a good man. There is a relish in good company and good things. As there is sweetness in the best things, so there is something in the children of God that is answerable to the God whom they serve. He is never so out of taste but he findeth his chief comfort in this thing, and he is never himself so much as when he is conversant in these things, though in different measure: sometimes more, and sometimes less. There is an inward antipathy to God in a proud carnal man that hath not his heart subdued by grace; there is a contrariety to the power of that grace which outwardly he professeth, and a sympathy with the world and the spirit of the world. Take a good Christian at the worst, he is better than another at the best. I beseech you, therefore, examine our dispositions; how we stand affected to things of an higher nature than the things of the world; to spiritual things, how we can relish spiritual things, God's ordinances, and anything that is holy. Surely if there be the life of God and Christ in us, there will be a kind of connaturalness and suitableness of taste to the sweetness that is in holy things.

---

[1] That is, 'naughty' = wicked. — G.

The priority of Christ's relation to the Father

To come to the next, mark the order here, 'Go to my Father, and your Father.' We are the sons of God at the second hand. God is the Father of Christ first, and then ours. He is his God first, then our God.

This is a weighty point for directing of our devotions, that we may know in what order to look on God. See God in Christ; see all things in Christ first, and then in us. Look upon him as Father to Christ, and then to us. Look on him as a God to Christ first, and in Christ a God to us. Look on him as having elected us, but elect in Christ first. See ourselves justified, but see Christ justified first from our sins, and his justification declared by his resurrection. See our resurrection and ascension, and glorification in heaven, not directly, but in Christ our head, who is in heaven, and taketh up place for us. See God loving us, but look on it in Christ, who is *sedes amoris.*[1] The next thing to God is his Son, and he loveth none but in him. When we consider of any spiritual blessing, say with the apostle, 'Blessed be God, that hath filled us with all spiritual blessings in Christ' (Eph. 1:3). Otherwise we do not know ourselves nor God. Whatsoever is derived from God to us is through Christ. All promises are his first. They are made to him, and to our nature in him, and they are performed for his sake. He taketh them from God the Father, and they be performed for his sake. He is the true Aaron,

---

[1] That is, 'seat of love'. — G.

We are but the skirts. The oil that is poured upon his head runneth down to his skirts. It runneth to the meanest Christian; but the ointment of grace is first poured on his head. 'Of his grace we receive grace for grace, and of his fulness' (John 1:16). The first fulness is God himself; the second receptacle of all is Christ, God-man; the third are we; we have it at the third hand. God emptieth himself into Christ, as mediator. In him are the fulness of all riches, the treasures of all wisdom and knowledge. We are completed in him, and in him we are full. His is not only a fulness of the vessel, as ours is, but a fulness of the fountain.

And it is for our comfort that it is so, that God's love is to Christ first. There is a firm foundation when God loveth us in his Son, and we are children in his natural Son, in whom we are adopted. Then our state is firm. Our first state in the first Adam was not firm, but now our nature is taken into the unity of the second person, it is firm. So that the love and care and fatherly disposition of God towards us, it is sweet to us, because it is tender to his Son. It is eternal to us, because it is eternal to him. He can as soon cease to love his Son, as cease to love us. For with the same love he loveth all Christ mystical, head and members. There is not the least finger of Christ, the least despised member of Christ, but God looketh on him with that sweet eternal tenderness with which he looketh upon his Son, preserving the prerogative of the head. Oh, this is a sweet comfort, that now all the excellent privileges of a Christian are set on Christ and then on us; and therefore we should not lose them, for Christ will lose nothing. When the favour of a prince is founded on his son whom he always loveth, the affection is unalterable on the son, and therefore the case is good. So God's favour to us is founded on his love to his Son, and therefore unalterable and eternal. We should therefore look up to God in his Son; put up all our petitions to him in his Son; expect all from him in his Son. He is in heaven for us, to do that that belongeth to us. Expect all from God through Christ, and do all to God through Christ; love God in Christ, and Christ in God; ourselves in Christ, and ourselves in the love of God. Christ is in God, and God is in Christ. God and Christ are in us. There is a marvellous sweet relation and communion between God and us, and Christ and us. It is a sweet communion, and mysterious to us. How sweet is the communion between the soul and the body, the soul being so spiritual, and the body a piece of earth! But what is this to the mystery of mysteries, when God takes clay and dust into unity of his person; and all this is for this union. The great and glorious union of Christ to our natures is that he may take us into his mystical body, and so make us one with himself, and one with the Father. He took our natures that he might convey his fatherly goodness and love and Spirit to us. The sweet union of the two natures of Christ is to confirm union between the Father and us, and Christ and us. And we are never happy till we be assured that we are one with Christ, which is the issue of his excellent prayer (John 17).

Our blessed Saviour fetcheth the comfort of our Father from this, that God is his Father first, and so to join both together; that God is our God, because he is his God first. It is a point very considerable, that whatsoever comfort we look for from God, and in God, we must see it in Christ first before we see it in ourselves, because we be but sons by adoption, and we have all we have from God through Christ. Whatsoever we see in Christ, think this will belong to us. And whatsoever we look should belong to us, see it first in him. As verily as he ascended, we shall ascend; as verily as he rose, we shall arise; as verily as he is at God's right hand, we shall be there too; for by faith we sit now in heavenly places with Christ; and 'we shall judge the world, and be for ever with the Lord' (1 Cor. 6:3). Whatsoever we see in Christ, interest ourselves in it. And therefore we must not conceive of Christ as a severe person, but conceive of ourselves in union and communion with Christ our head; and to conceive of Christ as our head and surety, and 'second Adam', and as a quickening spirit, that communicateth all to us. And therefore when we are to deal with God, be sure to go through Christ; as we expect all from God through Christ, so give all to God through Christ again. Be sure to take Benjamin with us when we go; and come clothed with the garments of our elder brother, and do not doubt when we come with Christ, for else we dishonour Christ. Shall I come in the sweet name and mediation of my Saviour, that hath perfected salvation, and not be accepted of God, when God hath ordained him for that purpose? If we stagger, and doubt to receive anything at God's hand, we wrong not only God's bounty, but Christ the mediator. Carry this therefore all along with us. Do all in him, and desire God to pardon all for his sake, and God will regard us.

Use. Let us therefore make use of it, and add this further, that *if so be God is first the Father of Christ before he is our Father, and first the God of Christ before he is our God, and that all our good is dependent upon what God is to Christ first, then doth not this follow from hence, that we should not only thank God for ourselves, but thank God for whatsoever he hath done to Christ; not only comfort ourselves in it, but let God have the glory of it?* And this the Spirit of God in the holy apostles Peter and Paul led them to. (Eph. 1:3), 'Blessed be the God and Father of our Lord Jesus Christ.' What, and nothing but so? Nay, with a reduplication, 'Blessed be God the Father of our Lord Jesus Christ', even because he is the Father of our Lord Jesus Christ; because out of his infinite depth of wisdom and goodness he hath found out a way to save us in Christ, to be a Father to him, and in him a Father to us. It is said of the Virgin Mary, 'All generations shall call her blessed' (Luke 1:48). Why? Because she was the mother of the person that was God; she was the mother of Christ in human nature, and of God, because we may not sever the persons. And shall we bless the Virgin Mary, as mother of God, and not God as Father of Christ? If she be the mother of Christ-man, then God is the Father of whole Christ; and therefore blessed be God, not only that he is our Father and our God, but that he might be thus with satisfaction to divine justice, he hath found out such a way to be the Father of Christ; and Christ, as man, is an object of God's love and predestination as well as we. We deserved nothing at God's hands, but he found out such a way by taking the nature of man into unity of his second person, and so became a Father of Christ and of us. And therefore bless God, who hath predestinated Christ to be the Lamb of God, that hath freed him from sin, and set him at his right hand, raised him from the dead; that hath carried him into heaven, and ordained him to be Judge of quick and dead. Are these things severed from us? No. They be favours that be ours in Christ; his first, then ours. And therefore whensoever we think of anything Christ hath of his glory in heaven, as he is king of heaven and earth, and hath all power committed to him, glorify God for it, and think of it, This is mine; he is mine husband, my head; he hath taken up that glory, and whatsoever is in heaven, and enjoyeth them, he hath taken it up for me, and therefore we should bless God for it. So the apostle Peter: 'Blessed be God the Father of our Lord Jesus Christ, that hath begot us again to an inheritance immortal, undefiled, that fadeth not away, reserved in the heavens' (1 Pet. 1:3, 4). He hath begot us to a lively hope, 'through the resurrection of Christ from the dead'. So it is from the resurrection of Christ from the dead that Christ saith, 'God is my Father and your Father.' Since God's justice is satisfied by my resurrection; that is, declared to be satisfied; 'I ascend to my Father, and your Father; to my God, and your God.' I beseech you, let us not lose the comfort of these things, since our Saviour Christ intended them for comfort.

Christ's God and ours

To come to the words. First, Christ saith, God was his God, and our God, because his God. In what sense is God Christ's God? As mediator, as man, both in regard of his person and in regard of his office, God is Christ's God every way. See Psalm 22:9, which is a psalm of Christ, David being but a type of him in it: 'Thou art my God from my mother's womb'; and so God is Christ's God in his particular person, from his mother's womb.

(1.) For, first, *God was Christ's God when by his Holy Spirit he sanctified him in his mother's womb, and brought him out into the world.* Let the foolish disputes of friars, and dreams, and dotages of dunsical times[1] go. 'But thou art my God from my mother's womb.' And

(2.) *He is Christ's God, because he saved him from the massacre of the infants.* Our Saviour Christ makes

---

[1] That is, 'foolish thoughts of stupid times'.—P.

that prayer in Psalm 22, Mark 15:34, on the cross, 'My God, my God, why hast thou forsaken me?'

(3.) *God was Christ's God in protecting of him in his young time*, and afterward in going along with him still to his death; and in death, 'My God, my God' still. He would own God to be his God still; when God had deserted him to his sense and feeling, yet 'My God' still. So God was Christ's God, as Christ was man. Take Christ as mediator, God is the God of Christ; for God the Father hath by his authority put on Christ whatsoever he hath. The Father hath sent him into the world; the Father 'sealed' him; the Father sent him out as a propitiation for our sins; the Father hath declared him and 'anointed' him; and all these terms of authority, whereby the Father hath showed himself to be Christ's God, even in his office of mediatorship. So in regard of the care of his person from his mother's womb, and for ever; and in regard of his office as mediator he might well say, 'I go to my God.' In regard of the intimate familiarity and acquaintance maintained even on the cross, he might say, 'My God.'

But the comfort of it lieth in the second clause, that as God is the God of Christ, so he is our God, because he is the God of Christ.

What is it to be a God to any? In a word, to be a God is to be all-sufficient to any; to be sole-sufficient, and to be self-sufficient.

To be a God is to be all-sufficient for every creature;

to be all-sufficient when nothing else can be sufficient. And to be self-sufficient, to be sufficient of himself, and therefore to reduce all back again to himself. Now, God is a God of himself, for himself, and by himself. God is all-sufficient, self-sufficient, sole-sufficient; and whatsoever the creature hath, it hath it from him. There is, in a word, in God a sufficiency for all good and happiness, and an efficiency to apply that sufficiency for the good of the creature. And in particular to be a God to any, is to do for a creature that no creature in the world can do but God. To make it of nothing, to free it from misery that it is beset withal, when no other can free it, to recover it again. God is Jehovah, that hath a being of himself, giveth being to the creatures, that can make the creature of nothing, and being something, can make it nothing.

Now, if God be a God to any, he is not only to give being to us, in a certain rank of creatures, as we are advanced above other creatures, as to have a being, or a life of growing, or a life of sense, or to advance us to a life of creatures endowed with reason, whereby we are common in that fashion with angels, and understand God himself. Alas! this were a poor privilege if it went no further than to set us in that rank of creatures, though a great favour. But considering us in a lapsed estate, it is a poor favour to leave us here. And therefore God is said to be our God now in a state of grace, when he advanceth us to an higher being and life than all this, a life of grace here and of glory hereafter; when out of his sovereignty and power he reduceth all to help forward his main end, the salvation of his in particular. So God is a God in peculiar of some that he taketh out of base mankind. There is a world taken out of the world, as Augustine useth to speak.[1] And thus he is a God not to bestow a life of grace and supernatural being here, but a glorious condition hereafter in heaven; and to make all things serviceable to that, that we may say, 'All is ours, because we are Christ's, and Christ is God's' (1 Cor. 3:22, 23). So that whatsoever befalleth a Christian, is serviceable and conducible to the main and last end. And that is for God to be God indeed, to make us his in Christ Jesus, to give us a new creation and a new state, better than the first.

Now, what is the foundation of this, that God is our God in the covenant of grace? We say it is founded on Christ. God is Christ's God, and then our God; and that is the reason why Christ is called 'Immanuel', which is as much as to say, as it is expounded, 'God with us'. Not only because when he took our nature on him, there was God and man in one person; but the meaning of the word is, Christ is Immanuel, 'God with us'; by being God in our nature, and satisfying divine justice in our nature, hath brought God the Father and us into a sweet covenant. So that God may be our God and our Father, notwithstanding his justice; because all is satisfied by Christ, who took our nature to die for us.

---

[1] Cf. remark under footnote on p. 98. It is the ground of his entire doctrine of predestination. — G.

Christ is Immanuel, because he hath made God and us one. So that God is our God, and not only so, but our Father in him. Thus you see how it cometh to pass that God is our Father by Christ, who came to bring us again to God, as his whole office was to bring a few that had been singled out of mankind to God again, from whom they fell; for we all had communion with God in Adam, but we lost it; and now must be brought again to God, which must be done by Christ, God and man.

Thus much for the foundation of the point, that God is Christ's God, and God in Christ is our God, to do all things for us, to bring us to an happy condition here and an everlasting happy condition in heaven.

The comfort in God being our God
We see here it is brought as a ground of comfort, and so indeed it is. And we may observe from hence, *that now by the resurrection of Jesus Christ, God is not only become a Father to us, but a God*. This is a ground of many comforts. 'Go, tell my disciples', now I am risen again; and therefore justice is satisfied; and now they may have lively hope of a better condition hereafter. For God is my God, that hath raised me up, and who will raise up mine too. So that now we are copartners with Christ, sharers with him in the fatherhood of God, and God is God in common with Christ and us.

This may well be brought as a ground of comfort. If there were any comfort in the world of sweeter efficacy than this, our Saviour would have sent it to his disciples.

Comfort being his main office and his main end, he would have the best comfort after his best resurrection. And he picks this from amongst them all, 'Go, tell them, I go to my Father, and their Father; to my God, and their God.' And therefore it is a pregnant comfort; and indeed no heart can conceive the comfort of it, that we have interest together with Christ in God, and with the Fatherhood of God. And both these the Scripture joineth together: (2 Cor. 6:18), 'I will be your Father, and your God.'

To unfold the comforts more, God is said to be our God in covenant in Christ. He is the God of Christ, and therefore of us, because he hath made himself over to us. A thing is said to be another man's when the title is passed to another man. Now, God hath as it were passed over himself to his believing children and members of Christ. He hath made over himself to them to be their God; as he was the God of Abraham, Isaac, and Jacob, and all the patriarchs, prophets, and apostles, so he is of every good, believing Christian to the end of the world. God maketh himself over to be theirs; and, as the Scriptures' style is, he is their portion and their inheritance; a blessed portion, a blessed inheritance, more to us than if all the world were ours, than if heaven were ours, than if ten thousand worlds were ours, for he is our God that can create millions of worlds more than this if it were needful. *Habet omnia, qui habet habentem omnia*: he hath all things that hath him in covenant that hath all things. And therefore when the Scripture saith, 'I go to their God', it implieth, I go to him that is all in all to them, that is larger than their hearts can be; for what heart can conceive the fulness of the comforts arising from hence, 'that God is our God'? Many know they need comfort of such a transcendent nature. The heart of man is so distrustful, so faithless, and the conscience is such a clamorous thing, and therefore he cannot think this is too much. I beseech you, therefore, do not lose the comfort of it, that in Christ God is our God; though we can say of nothing else, it is ours. Perhaps we cannot say, great houses are ours, or friends are ours, or inheritances ours. That is no matter. We can say, that is ours which is infinitely more than that. We can say, God is ours in Christ. Nay, being exhorted to say by the Spirit of faith, that God is ours in Christ, all things in the world are ours. As you have it in that place of Scripture, 'All things are yours.' Why? 'Because you are Christ's, and Christ is God's.' 'Whether things present, or things to come, Paul, Apollos, Cephas, life, death, all is yours; you are Christ's, and Christ is God's'; that is, all things must by a command from God conspire to make us happy: affliction, or Satan, or death, or trouble of conscience, or desertion, or everything to help us to heaven. The curse is taken away, and there is a blessing hid in everything that befalleth a Christian, to bring him to heaven. Therefore it is a comfort of infinite extent. All is yours, because God is yours.

You shall see the extent of the comforts further by retail, as it were. If God be ours, then all is ours too.

What be they? The Scripture telleth you, and I should spend too much time in unfolding of them.

1. If God be ours, his wisdom must needs be ours, to find out ways to do us good; for his infinite wisdom hath found out a way in Christ, by satisfaction of his justice, to bring us to heaven. He can make us go beyond all the policy of our neighbours, for his wisdom is ours.

2. If we [are] in danger, his power is ours, to bring us out.

3. If we have sinned, his mercy is ours, to forgive us. He himself being ours, his mercy must needs be ours. The whole being ours, it followeth out of the strength of reason that the parts also must be ours.

4. In any want, his all-sufficiency is ours, to supply it or to turn it to good, and make it up in a better kind.

5. In a word, God being ours, whatsoever is in God, whatsoever God can do, whatsoever he hath, is ours, because himself is ours. And therefore, I beseech you, make this use of it, to get into Christ by faith; to be one with Christ, that so God may be our God. Get faith above all graces, the grace of union and the grace of communion; that being one with Christ, we are one with him. God being ours, all is ours; yea, the worst thing in the world is ours.

If God be not ours, it is no matter what else is ours. Alas! all things must be taken from us, we know not how soon, and we taken from all things else. What if we had a kingdom, as Saul had, if we be forsaken of God as he was? What if we had paradise? If we offend God, we shall be cast out. What if we had the dignity to be apostles? If with Judas we have not God, what will all come to? What if a man enjoy all the world? If out of Christ, it would yield him no comfort! As the emperor said, I have gone through all varieties of condition, *et nihil mihi profuit*, but it hath done me no good.[1] If we had all, what is it but 'vanity of vanities'? and not only so, but 'vexation'? (Eccles. 1:2; 2:17). Now, when we have God to be our God, he is able to fill the soul. He is larger than the soul, and he is able to quiet the soul; he is the rest of the soul, the soul is quiet; in him is the centre, as the place of quiet. If God be ours, then the soul resteth in it; for God filleth the soul, and quiets the soul, and hath always fresh comforts for the soul, infinite still to all eternity. There is nothing in the world but we do as it were *deflorare*, take away the flower of it by use, and it becometh stale. Though a man continue many thousand years in the world, yet he will be weary of all things in the world, because there is no freshness in them. It is finite, and the soul is larger than the comforts of the world. But in God is a spring of fresh comforts to everlasting. Consider the things that enable him to be our God, to fill the soul, and to be larger than the soul; to quiet and calm the soul in all the troubles of

[1] 'As the heathen man said, that great emperor, "I have been all things, and nothing doth me good now", when he was to die.' '*Omnia fui, nihil expedit*' [I was all things; all was worthless] is ascribed to the emperor Septimus Severus on his death-bed (A.D. 211).—G.

it; and then to have fresh springs of comforts. What a comfort is this, to have God for their God!

Let it therefore raise up our souls to labour after God, and never rest till we have some interest in this great portion, of God to be our God. When we can by faith go out of ourselves to Christ, and lay a right and just claim to God to be our God, this is a comfort which reacheth from everlasting to everlasting. It giveth us forgiveness of sins when we had lost ourselves; because we are in Christ, he hath forgiven us. In all extremities and troubles, when no creature can comfort us, it is his glory to show himself a God. It reacheth to the resurrection of the body. God is Abraham's, and Isaac's, and Jacob's God when dead, because he was the God of whole Abraham, Isaac, and Jacob, and therefore of soul and body. And it reacheth from all favours of this world, so far as is for our good, to all eternity. Being our God, he will protect us from all extremities in this world; he will speak comfort to our souls, which nothing can do but God. When we be dead he will raise up our dust, because he is our whole God, the God of our souls and bodies, and we shall be for ever with the Lord. It is a comfort of wonderful extent.

Application
Use 1. God sovereign in our hearts
Let us therefore make this use of it. *Labour to make him so to us*; for as he is to us, so God by his Spirit

is our comforter, who being satisfied, giveth us his Spirit. We must make God our God, and then he will be a God to us. These be mutual wheresoever they be; wheresoever God is God to any, they by the Spirit obtained by Christ have grace to make him so to themselves. What is it for us to make God a God to us? It is this: to set up God a throne in our hearts; to give him a sovereignty over all things in the world, that we may say in truth of heart, God is our joy, God is our comfort, God is our rock, God is all in all to us. When we give him supremacy of affection above all the world, we esteem nothing above him; we value him above all esteem; his loving-kindness is better than life itself; for else we do not make him a God to us, and then it is no comfort to hear all the comforts spoken of before. For all to whom he is a God in the covenant of grace, and have hearts to make him so, the Spirit raiseth up their affections to make him a God to themselves. *Amor tuus, deus tuus*, as it is said of old, what we love most is our god. What we joy most in is our god, what we rely and trust in most is our god, as it was said of the 'wedge of gold' (Job 31:24). And therefore if anything hath our affections more than God, or equal with God, that we make our god. It is a query of the greatest concernment in the world to put to our hearts. What do I make my god? as David putteth the query to himself: 'Now, Lord, what is my hope? is it not in thee?' And so put this query to ourselves: Lord, what is my joy, what is my hope, what is my trust, what is my comfort? is it not in thee? If our hearts cannot make an answer to this in some sincerity, surely as yet we have not made God our God. Time may be that he may be so; but till by the Spirit of God we be brought to see an emptiness and vanity in the creature, and nothingness in all in comparison of God, that we can say, 'Whom have I in heaven but thee?' we have not comfort, because we do not make him ours by a spirit of mutuality. Where there is a covenant of grace there must be a mutual making of God our God, as he maketh himself to us.

Alas! we may be ashamed of it; the best do often forget themselves. Oh how do men value the favours of a man, and the promises of a man; the seal of a man for such and such a benefice; and how doth it grieve them to have the frowns of flesh and blood, the frowns of greatness! But when their consciences tell them they are under guilt of many sins, and God is not in good terms with them, how doth this affect them? And when their consciences cannot say they have promises sealed in Christ of the favours and mercies of God here and hereafter, alas! it is dead comfort: Ἐμοὶ τὸ παρὸν [*Emoi to paron*], Give me that which is present, and take you that which is to come, is the language of both. How few can say from sincerity of heart that they make good[1] to be their God? And therefore it is of greater concernment than we take it.

---

[1] Qu. 'god'? — Ed.

Use 2. God the ground of our obedience

As it is a ground and foundation of comfort, *so of all obedience to God*, as it is prefixed before the commandments, 'I am the Lord your God' (Exod. 20:2, 3), 'you shall have no other gods but me', and do all in obedience to me from this ground. But much more now. Then he was the Lord God that brought them out of Egypt; but now God may prefix, 'I am your Lord God in Christ', that have brought you from hell and damnation, that intend you heaven and happiness, and therefore do so and so. Since this is the spring of all obedience, we ought to labour to make it good, and often to examine ourselves, as before, what we make our god, and what we pitch our affections on. Alas! is our soul for anything but God? Hath not God made us for himself? and will our hearts rest in anything but God? Why then should we love vanity, and besot ourselves? When death comes, they may say, as Saul said, 'The Philistines are upon me, and God hath forsaken me' (1 Sam. 13:12). Death is on me; trouble, sickness, vexation of conscience is on me, and God hath forsaken me; I have no God to go to. What a miserable estate is this! And therefore, I beseech you, let us labour to have interest in the covenant of grace, to make it good that God is our God in Jesus Christ.

Who giveth us a being to be Christians, to have a new nature, to have a good being, but God? Who maintaineth and preserveth that being but God? And who keepeth and preserveth us till we get into a glorious being in heaven but God, who is all-sufficient, self-sufficient, sole-sufficient, only-sufficient? This God is our God now in Christ.

God is to us in a more special singular manner than to other creatures, because he hath raised us to be a more excellent being, not only as men, we being in the highest rank of creatures next the angels; and so he is a God to us more than to inferior creatures that have a more circumscribed and narrow being. Man hath a large being, a reasonable soul, and is fitted by nature to have communion with God, who is wisdom itself, and with angels; but all this were little comfort unless we had higher degrees of being than this. If God be our God in Christ, we have a spiritual being, which is as much above the dignity and prerogative of our ordinary being as our being by nature is above the basest creature in the world. And so God setteth a style upon us suitable to the excellency of our spiritual being. There is nothing excellent in the world but we are termed by it now, to set out the advancement and excellency of the dignity we have from God in a special manner; to be 'sons', 'jewels', his 'portion', his 'diadem', to be whatsoever you can imagine that is glorious and excellent: an excellent condition, though spiritual and concealed from the world. God's children are concealed men, as you shall see afterward. They be hidden men. The world taketh no notice of them, because their excellency is seen with another eye than the world hath. 'The God of the world blindeth the eyes of worldlings' (2 Cor. 4:4). They cannot see into the excellency of God's children, no more than they know God himself and Christ himself. So you see what it is to be a God in nature and in grace; to be all in all unto us; to have our whole substance and dependence in him. 'In him we live, move, and have our being', and well-being.

In this our excellency consisteth, that God is our God in Christ, who was God; and that he might bring God and us to good terms together; that he might make God our God. He was Immanuel, God with us, to make God with us in favour and love. The Godhead is nearest the human nature of Christ of any creature. It is nearer to Christ than to the angels; for God hath not taken the angels into hypostatical union, to be in the same person; but God in Christ is so near our nature, that there is an hypostatical union. They make one person, our nature being taken into the second person. By reason of this near union of the Godhead to our nature cometh that comfort and near union between God and our nature, whereby God hath sweet communion with us in Christ. God by his Spirit, though not hypostatically, yet graciously, is one with us, and hath communion with us now as his children. So that sweet intercourse between God and us now, is founded upon the nearness of the Godhead to our nature in Christ, in whom it is nearest of all, in whom it is advanced above the angelical nature. And therefore our blessed Saviour might well say, 'I go to my God, and your God'; to his God first, and then to our God.

Now we may say, God is our God; and upon good grounds, because God is Christ's God, and in him our God, which is a point of singular comfort; and therefore I will enlarge myself further in it.

Doct. For God to be our God, especially in having that in our hearts unfolded, in regard of our spirits and best being, is the most fundamental comfort that we have. For from this, that God is our God, cometh all that we have that is good in nature and grace. Whatsoever is comfortable cometh from this spring, that God in Christ is our God, our reconciled God; that God's nature and ours now are in good terms.

Beloved, what cannot we expect from God, that is now become our God! What he is, what he is able to do, what he hath, all is ours, considering himself is ours. If we have the field, we have the pearl in the field. And therefore the wise merchant in the gospel sold all for the field wherein the treasure was (Matt. 13:44). We have the field itself in having God, and we have all that God is or can do for us for our good, even as we have Christ, and all that Christ is, or hath done, and suffered, and enjoyeth; 'all is ours, because we are Christ's, and Christ is God's,' as the apostle saith. So that having God we have all, because we have him that possesseth all, the creator of all, and preserver of all, and disposer of all.

But to clear the objection a little: if God be ours, and all things else, how comes it that we want so many things?

Ans. I answer, It is our own fault for the most part. We want faith to make use of and improve this comfort. And then again, we want nothing that is for our good; want itself is for our good. And observe this, our God is so powerful a God, that he maketh the worst things we suffer a means to convey the greatest good oftentimes to us. If God be our God and Father in Christ, why have we sins? Why vexed with the devil? Why persecuted with men? Why frightened thus, and thus, and thus? All this is for our good. God is our God by these, and in the midst of these; and is never more our God than in the greatest extremity of all, for then we come nearest the fountain. There is a near and sweet communion between this God and us, when we take of the fountain. When the means are drawn away, the conduits of conveyance, and we have nothing to go to but God immediately, there is sweet communion and sweetest comfort in heaven; we shall have God in Christ, who will be all in all unto us. We shall need no magistracy, ministry, food, raiment, or defence against cold or injury; we shall be out of the reach of Satan and all enemies; God will be all in all immediately. The same God is all in all to us, either by means or immediately. When means fail, he conveyeth his sweetness and his power immediately, but ordinarily by means. And what sight doth in heaven, faith doth now in some proportion; for as sight in heaven seeth God in Christ all in all, and enjoyeth that happy vision, so faith seeth God to be all in all, and Christ to be all in all. Though in an inferior degree to sight and clearness of vision, yet for the capacity of this life we enjoy God now as they do in heaven. We have inward comforts when most deserted. God was never more near our blessed Saviour than on the cross, when he cried, 'My God, my God' *etc.*, for then he found invincible strength supporting him in the great undertaking under the wrath of his Father. And so God is never nearer than in extremity; in strength, though not in sense and feeling; and oftentimes in feeling itself. We never have sweeter comforts than in the want of all outward comforts whatsoever, when nothing else can comfort us but the presence of God. And we must know besides, that the state of a Christian in this world is an hidden condition; for it is to the eye of faith, not of sense; and therefore God is a God to his, though the world see it not. There is a secret, hidden influence, a secret passage between heaven and earth, that none seeth. Who observeth the influence of the sun, or the sweet influence of the stars upon the earth? Light we see, but there is a secret influence pierceth deeper than the light, to the very bowels of the earth, whence metals come. Where no light comes, there is an influence, though not discerned; and much more can there be influence of strength and power and hidden comfort, though there be no sight. Cannot God be our God in regard of strength, supporting and supplying, though there be no visible and sensible comfort, though we see it not ourselves? Certainly the soul is upheld by an invincible strength in the worst condition that can be. Therefore this is true, that God is our God in all conditions.

Use. Let us make use of this. To what use is riches and friends, if we do not use them? To what use is God and Christ, if we use them not? *Nostrum est, utamur nostro bono.* He is ours, let us use him for our special good on all occasions. Oh that we had faith answerable to our prerogative. It is a prerogative more than heaven and earth, that God is ours; and had we faith suitable, what kind of persons should we be in grace and comfort, and whatsoever is good? Therefore labour to make use of it. But more of this after we have spoken of some rules of trial, because whatsoever I may say this way may be misapplied. They be excellent comforts. But perhaps, saith the distressed soul, they belong not to me, to whom it doth belong. Perhaps it belongeth to me, saith another that is a stranger and a carnal man, to whom it doth not belong. Therefore our Saviour giveth some notes of distinctions, to know whether God be our God or no. Not to be much in the argument, yet to be plain in it.

(1.) *God is their God in this peculiar manner I speak; that is, in the covenant of grace, not otherwise*; and I speak not what God is by creation of man, for so the devil is God's, and every creature. But the question is, Whom God is a God to in the nearest bond of the covenant of grace? That is the only comfortable relation that can be; for if God be not our God in that, all other comforts will be nothing. It is better we be no creatures at all, than not creatures in the covenant of grace. It is therefore worthy the commending to you, especially considering our naughty hearts are prone to deceive us. Satan, and melancholy, and temptations do make some refuse the comfort, and some presumptuous persons to snatch at it when it doth not belong to them. Those to whom God is a God indeed, in a sweet relation of the covenant of grace to be their God, as to the patriarchs, prophets, and Christ and the apostles, he giveth his Holy Spirit to witness so much to them. Though the voice of the Spirit is not always heard in the best children of God, yet he giveth them the Holy Spirit, that though it doth not always witness, yet it always works something in them which may be an evidence that they are God's.

(2.) Now the spirit of adoption and sonship is known *by a spirit of supplication especially*. Whom God is a God to, he vouchsafeth a spirit of prayer, to go to him in all their necessities, which is an issue or branch of their faith. He giveth them faith to believe it, and prayer to make use of it; for God will not give this great privilege without hearts to make use of it, which is done by faith and prayer; and prayer is nothing but the frame of faith (Acts 9:11). As soon as Paul was a good man, presently after his conversion, 'behold he prayeth'. The child crieth as soon as born, and the child of God is known by his praying; as soon as he is converted, an intercourse is opened between God and the soul, which a Christian soul will never neglect. If they are placed in the worst condition, they will pray to God, or at least sigh and groan, which is a prayer that God can make sense of. Those that have any strong places of defence, in trouble they will be sure to fly to that; in times of war they will betake them to their castle and place of munition. And so they that be God's, in time of danger run presently to God; he is their rock, their refuge, and place of defence. [They] repair to him by faith and prayer. 'The name of the Lord is a tower of defence: the righteous in trouble fly thither, and they are safe' (Prov. 18:10). A man may know what his god is by his retiring in times of extremity. Your carnal man, if he hath any place to retire to, it is to his friends, to his purse, to bring him out. He will go to that which his instinct will specially lead him to in times of trouble. As every creature, together with the nature of it, hath received an instinct from God to go to the place of refuge wherein it is safe – as the weakest creature hath strongest refuge – the conies, a poor weak creature, hide themselves most strongly, out of instinct they have of their own weakness – so God's child, being privy of his weakness, and need of support and strength, hath the strongest support that may be, and runneth to his God. Worldly men have many shifts, as the wily fox hath; but a Christian hath but one, but that is a great one: he goeth to his God in time of need. And therefore you may know who is in covenant with God in times of extremity, especially by a spirit of faith, a spirit of prayer.

In times of extremity, no man but a Christian can pray with any comfort, with any sweet familiarity, 'Abba, Father'; but they be like Pharaoh, 'Go, Moses, pray to your God' (Exod. 9:28). He hath no such familiarity with God as to pray for himself. And so carnal men will say, 'Pray to your God.' And many, like devils, will have no communion with God in their prosperity, but their whole life is a provoking of God to enmity, by swearing, loose, debauched, irregular carriage, hateful even to moral men. Their hearts tell them they be even like Satan, 'What! dost thou come to torment us before our time?' (Matt. 8:29). What hast thou to do with me? What have they to do with God? They have scarce a Bible in their chambers; if one, it is for fashion's sake. And that they may not appear to be naught, they will hold conformity in public assemblies; but for private familiarity, they have nothing to do with it. The show of religion goeth under an opprobrious name, but if they would put off the show it were nothing, and not make ostentation of what they are not; but they have no communion with God in prayer. They will go for God's people, and own him for their God, when they have no trading with him so much as by prayer. Take heed we deceive not ourselves, I beseech you; salvation dependeth upon it.

(3.) We may further try *whether our claim of God to be our God be a good claim, on good grounds, by our siding, by our part-taking*; for those whom God is a God to in a peculiar manner will be sure to side with God. God hath two things in the world he prizes more than all the world; that is, his children and church, his cause and religion. They that be God's will be sure to side with the church, they will stand and fall with the church; and the cause of religion, they will live and die with it. But a carnal politician, that hath perhaps great parts of nature, he is Ἀλλὰ πρὸς αλλοῦς [*Alla pros allous*], as the Grecian calleth him; they be for all turns; they can bring themselves to any figure, like water that will receive any figure.[1] Take it, put it into a vessel that is square, it will be square; put it into a round vessel, it will be round. How can they own God for their God when they will not seek him, and they are yet to choose their God and religion? And because they will be sure to be safe in all times, they will own no religion in any time. And, beloved, is it possible any such should say with confidence, God is their God? Will he own them

---

[1] 'Like to the Samaritans, as Josephus, the historian of the Jews, writes of them. When the Jews prospered, oh! then they would be Jews', *etc.* The passage will be found in the *Antiquities*, Book ix., c. xiv. § 3, 'When they [the Cutheans or Samaritans] see the Jews in prosperity, they pretend that they are changed, and allied to them, and call them kinsmen, as though they were derived from Joseph, and had by that means an original alliance with them; but when they see them falling into a low condition, they say they are no way related to them, and that the Jews have no right to expect any kindness or marks of kindred from them, but they declare that they are sojourners that come from other countries.' Cf. also xi. c. viii. §6, and xii. c. v. 5.—G.

that will not own him, nor his church, nor his cause? You know Jehu crieth out, 'Who is on my side, who?' Cast her out. And so God, in doubtful times of danger, crieth out, 'Who is on my side, who?' Stand out; appear, if you be on my side; if you be on my side, own my cause; if you be not on my side, if you have no degree of goodness, it will appear. Christian wisdom is one thing, carnal policy is another thing. 'The wisdom of the flesh is enmity with God' (Rom. 8:7). Many applaud, and think themselves for somebody in this kind; but this wisdom is enmity itself against God. When a man will be wise in a distinct kind of wisdom from God, when he will have a cause severed from God, and will not side with God, he must look that God will account him his enemy, and make him his; but especially in the hour of death and deep extremity, he shall not be able to look God in the face, to whom he hath been a traitor in the church and in the cause of religion. And therefore, as we will be able to own God for our God, especially in doubtful and dangerous times, side with the church, and side with religion. It was objected to that good Jehonadab, a good man, 'Have we anything to do with God's enemies?' (Jer. 35:6, *seq.*). Now there be two sorts of enemies that we are especially to have nothing to do withal if we side with God: enemies within us, and enemies without us. Sin within us. We must take part against our sins; take God's part and the Spirit's part against corrupt motions and affections. Divinity must begin from within, else it is faction without. It is not religion, but faction, if the religion begin not in our hearts, and if we hate not sin in ourselves. Where there is true antipathy, the nearer anything is that is opposite to our nature, the more hateful it is. He that hateth a toad, hateth it in his bosom most of all. And he that hates sin as sin, hates it in his own heart most of all. And therefore they that will pretend religion, and be naught in their own particular, it cometh not from a true principle; for they that will side with God, side with God in their own hearts, and be good men in their own particulars. Therefore, I beseech you, try yourselves by this. Likewise, when men esteem God's enemy wheresoever they see it, and so far as their authority and power reacheth, they will take God's part in themselves against themselves, and in the world too. I will not enlarge the point, because it cometh in by way of trial, and I cannot but touch it as a trial. Thus you see how we may know whether we be God's or no, by owning his cause and siding with him. You have some expressions in Scripture to this purpose: Micah 4:5, 'All people will walk every one in the name of his god, and we will walk in the name of the Lord our God for ever and ever.' Every man will walk and converse in the name of his god; they will own their god and take part with him; and we will walk in the name of our God for ever and ever, and own his cause at all times, and constantly, for ever and ever.

And likewise in Isaiah 44:5, speaking of gracious times there, when men shall be bold for the Lord, as in all times some men will. 'One shall say, I am the Lord's, and another shall call himself by the name of Jacob, and another shall subscribe with his hand to the Lord, and term himself Israel.' God shall have his tongue, his hand, and all. He shall say, 'I am the Lord's,' he shall call himself 'by the name of God', he shall subscribe to it, and own the cause.

(4.) Again, If we would know whether God be our God, *we must know whether we may lay just claim to our God as a peculiar God to us, or no, and that way in which God showeth himself to be a God in peculiar respects to us.*

Quest. Now how doth God show himself a God in a peculiar respect to his children?

Ans. He showeth himself to have a peculiar respect to them, –

[1.] *By peculiar gifts, when he gives to them that which he giveth to none else.* Shall we imagine God to be our God by common gifts and common graces? No. For thou comest to hear the word; so Herod did. Thou receivest the sacrament; so did Judas, so did Simon Magus. Thou hearest the truth with some joy; so did the 'third ground' (Matt. 13:20). Thou hast excellent parts; so hath the devil himself.

But thou art in such a place of the church, teachest others; so did Judas. Are these evidences to try whether we be God's or no? What then is the peculiar gift and love-token that God bestows upon his favourites? They be the graces of his Spirit, especially in regard of God:

an humble, broken heart, and a believing heart, and a lowly heart, that goeth out of itself, that goeth unto God by faith, and towards man full of love, which argueth a great deal of self-denial, when a man can love others with denial of his own profit and ease. He that hath a humble, believing, lowly heart, hath more than all the world besides, for he hath God's peculiar gift. Many poor souls complain as if God had no regard to them, and yet in the mean time they have humble, broken hearts, which is more than if they had all the wealth and worth that the world hath, which have proud hearts, never broken. The return of these favours will be comfort in death and glory in heaven. What will the fruit of a believing heart be? He hath God and Christ. If he hath a lowly, large heart to do good, he doth that which in the issue shall further his account at the day of judgment; and there is the love of God showed in his special favour.

[2.] *So the love of God especially shall be a peculiar comfort that the world is ignorant of, especially in times of extremity.* Inward peace of conscience, inward joy, and inward comforts, these are signs of love that God bestoweth upon a man, when he will own him in the worst times, and speak peace to his soul when nothing in the world will speak peace. When the lions roar, [when] the great lions of the world roar in extremity, he hath inward peace and joy, and comforts of the Holy Ghost. That inward intercourse of God with the soul is a sign of God's peculiar love. When God speaketh peace to the soul, when he showeth the light of his countenance, which David in Psalm 4:7 prefers before all outward comforts whatsoever – God's revealing of himself, as the Scripture calleth it – when God revealeth himself to his to be theirs, with peace, and joy, and comfort accompanying it, this is peculiar.

[3.] Again, A peculiar favour and love-token of God *is to have seasonable and sanctifying correction.* To have corrections when they be seasonable; when we be in a way of straying, and God will bring us home by correction; and when we have sanctified correction, we find by experience that all is turned to our good. If I find anything turn me to my God, I know I am his; if my cross be seasonable and sanctified, he is my God, for he takes that course with me which he takes with his own people. These be singular signs of God's love, when he bestoweth the graces of his Spirit, his comforts, peace, and joy, though not largely, yet so much as shall sustain the soul. And then, when he seasonably meeteth us, and will not suffer us to thrive in an evil course. Oh it is a judgment of judgments to be hardened in sinful courses of life; how can it but end in desperation at length? And therefore it is a great favour to be chastised; it showeth 'we are sons, and not bastards'. Thus we see how we may lay just claim to this, that God is our God in a peculiar manner.

(5.) To name but one more, to distinguish a spirit of presumption from a spirit of faith and truth, that God is our God, is this,

[1.] *If we have grace to answer his dealings towards us*, when we can echo to God's dealings. God hath chosen us, if we have grace to choose him for our God. We may know he hath called us effectually, when we answer God's call. When he biddeth us believe, he giveth an influence of power to be able to say, 'I believe; Lord, help my unbelief' (Mark 9:24). We may know he loveth us, when we reflect love again, and love him. We may know he compasseth us, when we embrace him. We may know he delighteth in us, when we delight in him and his servants. Whence is the strength of this argument? From hence. All good things, whatsoever we do, is from God, is by reflection. God shineth on us first; God owneth us for his first, and God must do so in order of causes. God being the spring of all goodness, he must begin. 'We love him because he loved us first' (1 John 4:19), else we could never love him. Therefore if we love him and truth, he loveth us. That is sure. 'What have I in heaven but thee, and in earth of comparison of thee?' (Psa. 73:25). Surely he owneth us, because in order of causes we can have nothing but from him first.

[2.] And then again, *out of the nature of conscience; if we can go boldly to him as a reconciled God, notwithstanding guilt of conscience*, it is a sign he hath obtained peace of conscience, because it is the nature of conscience, if it hath not peace from God, not to dare to appear in God's presence. So then, when there is inward peace and love answering to God's love, choice answerable to God's choice, apprehending of him answerable to his apprehension, this reflection, and return, and rebounding back to God, is an invincible argument that God hath first shined upon that soul. God sometimes will let us see things in the effect, and hide them in the cause. Perhaps he will not persuade by his Spirit that he loveth us, hath chosen us, and that we are his; but he will work something in our hearts, because he will have us search our spirits, what good thing he hath wrought, what love, what choice of the best side are in any of these. Surely then God is theirs. Though there be not an open voice, yet they may know God hath loved this soul and spoken peace to that soul, because we can return nothing to God, but he must shine on us first.

Therefore, beloved, let us make use of this, and let us take heed of sacrilegious usurpations, that we do not usurp upon God's house or God in a peculiar respect. Indeed, we may come to God as his creatures – we are the workmanship of thy hands – and say the truth, though we be in a wicked course of life. But to say, 'Thou art my God in Christ', 'I am thine, thou hast chosen me for thine', when we have not chosen him for our God, nor loved him nor his cause, nor sided with him, nor have any stamp of him on the soul, have nothing but common favour, that castaways have as well as we, and the devils as well as we – for the devils go beyond all men in parts – and yet to usurp the prerogative of being God's in a peculiar manner, and to be bold with the holy things of God, as if we were of his family, this is a dangerous usurpation; take heed of it. And therefore they that live in courses of rebellion, and resolve not to mend, they take the holy things of God, as the psalmist speaks (Psa. 50:16, 17), in an holy indignation, 'What art thou, that takest my word in thy mouth, since thou hatest to be reformed?' Thou art an enemy to God and goodness, and wilt be so; thou art in a course of rebellion, and wilt be so. The devil's works you do and will do. Can we not take the word of the covenant into our mouths, and shall we take the seal of the covenant? Therefore resolve to amend, else have nothing to do with God; do not add one sin to another. 'It is the children's food, and not for dogs' (Matt. 15:26); it belongeth to them of the family. If thou be none of the family, what hast thou to do with them? If thou be of the family, whatsoever thy infirmities are, thou mayest come boldly, for the seals are to strengthen our weak faith. When the father is father of a child, the father will not cast away the child for breaking out with deformity or lameness. When God hath taken us into his family, infirmities cannot discard us. But I speak of them that in a wilful opposite course of sin show they never had to do with God in familiar intercourse. God never gave them a spirit to alter their natures. Propriety,[1] and proportion, and suitableness of disposition go together: propriety joineth with suitableness; where God owneth any man, he makes them like himself by his word and Spirit, that their natures shall be even and agreeable to holy things, shall have a taste

---

[1] That is, 'property or ownership'.—Ed.

of holy things. And where there is not suitableness of holy things, there is no propriety. Will God own a man, and not make him suitable? Will God take his friend, and not give him a friendly nature? He will not, for he first fitteth our natures for communion with himself, else there can be no propriety. Let us not deceive ourselves, but if we find some beginnings of grace, and can say without arrogancy or usurpation, 'Doubtless thou art our Father, our God' (Isa. 63:16); we be not worthy to be thine, but we be thine; if we find something that castaways cannot have, some grief of heart for sin, some faith, some little measure of love, some love of truth and inclination to the best things, then we may come boldly to increase our familiarity and communion with God. But otherwise it is dangerous to come to God. We approach 'a consuming fire' (Heb. 12:29). 'Who shall dwell in everlasting burnings?' (Isa. 33:14). Say they in Isaiah, And if God be not in covenant with us, oh, he will be 'a consuming fire', everlasting burnings, and we but stubble; and it will increase spiritual judgment in us, hardness of heart, and going on from sin to sin, till we be accursed for sin. Therefore it is a fearful thing to be given up to hardness of heart. They that do continue in sin, God giveth them up to hardness of heart, to be insensible of his dealings with him.

Use 3. God all-sufficient for us

If we can in any degree make it good that God is our God and we his people, then let us make use of it for our comfort in all times, *that we have a God to go to*. Though we have no friend in the world, yet we have him in whom all friends meet. If we have no comfort here, yet we have him in whom all comforts meet, for all concentre in him. He hath father and friends, and worth and grace, and peace and comfort in him; and all is in him. If we go to him, we shall find a confluence of everything that is good, suitable to any necessity of ours.

And therefore let us learn to single out of God whatsoever may help us to be in covenant with him. He having made himself over to be ours, let us learn this wisdom, to single out of God whatsoever is peculiar to our present condition; for considering he hath made himself a God to us, he is all-sufficient to every turn. Therefore out of his all-sufficiency, take out whatsoever is fit for any particular exigency. 'Lord, I am in a strait, and want wisdom.' Thou in Christ hast abundance of wisdom. Christ hath in him all treasures. I now want friends, I want counsel, I want help, I want strength. God hath a fulness of all this for his children. He hath it not only to content himself, and look on his own happiness, but for his friends that be in covenant with him, that be so near him that he will own him to be their God. If you ask, What is religion? it is to know God, to have all-sufficiency in him for any good, and then to make use of him by dependence on him for that good, and by advancing of him in giving him the due honour and thanks of it. And therefore we deserve not the names of religious persons, if we do not study what he is to his creatures in the covenant of grace. Then make use of it by a spirit of dependency, and always giving praise and thanks. This is our whole man, and what is all else? Nothing but trouble and vanity. Get our bonds sealed that he is our God, and then break with all the world beside. Come what can come, or what will come, we are sure to be safe. It is a comfort of wonderful large extent. The use of the sacrament is to seal that God is our God in particular, and that Christ is ours as verily as the bread and wine are ours. And let us desire the Lord to seal to every one of our souls, that are to have communion with him in particular, that he in Christ is ours: Christ with all his merits and fruits of them, forgiveness of sin and life everlasting, as verily as the outward man partakes of the outward seals; and then we shall come and go away with comfort, and be made partakers of that end and use of the sacrament for which our blessed Saviour instituted it.

Having spoken before of common favours, which devils and castaways may have as well as we, I shall enlarge myself a little in this, because it is a point of concernment. As in other sins we be like the devil, so in this sin a man is worse than the devil himself, if a man will be a common swearer, and opposer, and malicious against goodness, being only in love with some idle conceit of his own, which he will have God himself stoop to else he will not to heaven; he will not be saved but by his own foolery. A man that hath a bitter spirit against the power of grace, that is a common blasphemer, that carrieth a spite against religion, for him to say, 'God is his God', the devil will as well say so. He will say of Paul and Silas, These are the people of God; but he will not say himself is (Acts 19:15). For a man to live in sins against conscience, defend them, oppose all that opposeth his sins, and yet claim an interest while that disposition standeth in him, it is more than satanical impudency, and it is extreme hardening of the heart against all goodness; for how many thousands in the church perish and sink to hell under this presumptuous conceit, 'I am God's, and God is mine', when the title is false, and the evidence false. And therefore it is a point deserving thoroughly to be examined continually, what those evidences of graces be that we venture our souls and salvation upon. I will not stand much to press the point. But you see the necessity of it. Consider therefore, I beseech you, what I have said. If God be ours, there will be a separation. Where there is an owning of God for their God, there will be a separation from all that is not his, as well as a gathering to them that be his. The work of God's Spirit in his children is like fire, which hath two properties: to sever all heterogeneal and strange stuff, and dross, and the like, and gather all the homogeneal stuff of one nature. And so the works of the Spirit gathereth to the soul so much as is good, and refines that, and severeth that which is contrary. The Spirit of God, that telleth them that they be God's, it is a severing Spirit and a uniting Spirit. It severs contraries, and it uniteth things of the same nature. There is a joining to what is good, and a separating of what is evil.

I will add this farther, that wheresoever on good title we can say, 'I am God's,' there is a reflect act of the soul to say, 'God is mine'. God hath put a light of reason and friendship into man. Now friendship standeth in mutual office of duty and gift. Where this is not, there is no friendship, no reconciliation, no owning on good terms. The end why God saveth a company of men, and bringeth them to heaven; the body of Christ, which we call the church; it is, that he may have eternal communion with them in the heavens, as he hath with the blessed angels; and in Christ a nearer communion than he hath with them. Now how can this communion be, unless we turn to God, unless we have something to answer God's love?

Again, Note, *God is ours, because Christ is ours*. The covenant is made first with Christ, and then with us. Whence we see a ground of particular application of that which we call particular faith; a ground of particular application by a Spirit of faith of God to us, and Christ to us; that God in Christ is my God and your God.

The ground of this is, as God offereth himself, we must apprehend him; but Christ offers God, and he knoweth how to offer him. He teacheth us how God is to be presented, and he presenteth him as our God and our Father; and therefore let us entertain him as ours. Thus you see a good ground of particular application of God the Father, and Christ to us in particular, in two respects; not only that everyone in particular ought to have a particular faith, and not to think a general faith is enough, to believe as the church believeth, but to have a particular faith of the object; not only of the subject, but of the object; that that is his in particular, 'I go to my Father and your Father.'

God is the Father and the God of all the elect, and only the elect, and of every one of the elect, as we say, *in solidum*. That is said to be *in solidum*, when every one applieth the whole to himself, without diminution of any part. The sum is *in solidum* to everyone that will make use of it, to enlighten every creature that shutteth not his eyes. As a common fountain is no man's in particular; for no man can say, This is my fountain, and yet every man can say, This is mine; so every saint can say of God, He is mine *in solidum*. Though he were alone, he may say, God is mine. If ten thousand have him, yet God is his God. God careth for all, as if there were but one, and for one, as if none but he. God offers himself, not only to his whole church, but to every one in particular, and therefore of every one he ought to be apprehended.

This is founded in all the great points and mysteries of religion. As for instance, what is the ground of all the petitions in the Lord's prayer? 'Our Father.' What interest have we to all the petitions, and to every article of the creed? If there be not a particular application, – 'I believe God the Father to be *my* God, Jesus Christ *my* Saviour, the Holy Ghost *my* sanctifier; remission of sins and life everlasting is mine' – we do no more than the devils. Now every truth in Scripture is written for our comfort, and shall it be no more comfort to us than to the devils? Doth the Scripture intend us no more comfort than the devils? Yes. But the devil may say, for the church there is remission of sins, and a God and Saviour, but not for me; and that is his torment; he cannot come to particulars. So the sacraments are to seal a particular faith. As every one in particular taketh the bread and wine, so by a particular faith everyone may say, Christ is mine; his death is mine; bloodshed mine; remission of sins and interest of Christ is mine. It doth not seal a general faith in the clouds, but a particular assurance, that it belongeth to everyone. And so in the words of the catechise,[1] the ministerial questioning of sinners is intended, that every one that believeth should apply it, If thou believest, and if thou believest, thou shalt be saved; and thy sins shall be forgiven thee. So that if we regard prayer and faith, if we regard the sacraments, or the use of the catechise, all enforce a particular faith. If we have not particular faith, we lose the virtue of all. So it is for the commandments. Put case, no man in particular, yet every one ought to ply in particular, that they ought to abstain from such a sin, and perform such a duty. If they do so, they shall be glorified; if not, they shall be punished. And there

---

[1] That is, the Church Catechism. —Ed.

is the same reason in faith as in obedience. A man is condemned in law, though not named in law; because the general is set down here, and every man ought particularly to apply it; I ought not to have done so and so. So that it overturneth the end of all, if a man labour not for a particular faith.

To go farther. Now if I disable this interest of particular faith of God's love, and Christ's love, I lose the comfort of weak faith where it is true. What condition were they in now, when Christ biddeth Mary go? Had not some of them denied Christ, and had they not all forsaken him? And yet notwithstanding, 'Go tell Peter', and tell them all, 'I go to their Father and their God'. So that the interest that a soul hath in Christ, who hath true faith, though a weak faith joined with many infirmities, the interest he hath in Christ is not broke off, as you see by the example of the apostles. And therefore I beseech you, let us comfort ourselves in this, labouring for a particular faith, and then labour to maintain our interest, notwithstanding our infirmities and faults, notwithstanding our sins past. Let not Satan rob us of our claim, that God is our God and Father in Christ. Let us learn of Christ; we cannot have a better pattern. What doth Christ on the cross, when he had the sins of all the believing world upon him, and had there been ten thousand times more, it had been all one to so infinite a person, God-man; he had made full satisfaction to God's justice. But having so much upon him, did it take away his claim of God, as his

God? It did not, but still he said, 'My God, my God'. Was it a claim that did him any good? Was it a useful claim? Yes. For it was made good by his resurrection and ascension; and therefore he might well say, 'I go to my God and your God.' I have overcome the wrath of God due for sin; and therefore when I, that had all the sins of the world upon me, acknowledged God to be my God, and underwent the burden of God's wrath, and satisfied for all sin, you may well say, '*My* God'; not only from the pattern of Christ, because he did so, but as a cause. I may say so now, because Christ said so then. For he hath fully satisfied his Father, who had laid that burden on him. You, therefore, that have particular burdens of your sins, and have not that other, but have a conscience troubling you, it is for good; because if you believe, that is taken away. But put case you had the guilt of your own sins, and many sins beside, what is that to this of Christ, who had the guilt of all sin? And therefore let no guile hinder you from a spirit of faith, to say, 'My Father, and my God.' Is Christ ascended to heaven, to be a mediator of intercession to appear before God? For whom? Is it not for sinners? What work is there in heaven for a mediator, if we were not daily sinners? Christ that hath satisfied for sin, biddeth us, after satisfaction, to think of God as a Father, and think of his ascension; even for this end to appear before God for us as our high priest, to make daily peace for us. His blood is of everlasting efficacy. And if Abel's blood cried for vengeance, the blood of Christ crieth for mercy (Heb. 12:24). As the appearing of the blood of Abel spake for vengeance, so the very appearing of Christ speaks enough for mercy to the sinner.

It is a comfortable clause that in Hosea 2:19, where God saith, 'He will marry them in everlasting mercy.' So that mercy is a part of the jointure of the church. God will marry them in mercy; in what mercy? In pardoning mercy; as the husband is to bear with the wife, the weaker vessel, not to put her away for infirmities. Shall we attribute mercy to men, and not to God? Can a friend bear the infirmities of a friend, and a husband of a wife? And cannot Christ bear the infirmities of his spouse? And therefore never think that our infirmities may hinder our claim. You see it did not here. But 'Go to my Father, and your Father.' This comfort we shall be driven to make use of some time or other, and therefore make use of it now.

But you will say, This is not comfort for common sort of Christians. It is not, and I intend it not for them. It is children's bread, and it must not be cast to dogs. Therefore they that have not God for their God, and live in any sin, they can lay no claim to him, for they serve another god in their hearts. Their vile courses are instead of their god, and in their affections above their God, and therefore let them not think any promise belongeth to them in that course. Let them think of God as 'a consuming fire', as 'everlasting burnings', while they be such, and that their peace is as the peace that the soul hath when the strong man holdeth all in possession;

when the conscience is speechless, and God hath given them up to hardness of heart, which is a desperate peace. This belongeth to them that are resolved not to live in any sin, that have given themselves up to God; and yet by reason of the remainder of corruption are driven to make use of that petition which Christ bids them to pray, 'Forgive us our daily sins.'

Assurance of salvation

Use 1. Hence issueth this truth, *that a Christian may be assured of his salvation in this world*. For, first of all, grant that we ought particularly to apply, as God offers himself to us, and that no infirmities nor sins hinders this claim, then what followeth but a Christian, believing and repenting of his sins daily, may be assured that he is in a state of grace, because there be grounds of particular application. That, therefore, which seems to disable that interest, hinders not at all. And therefore labour to maintain that comfortable state of assurance by all means. The grounds of it is, particular application, notwithstanding of all sins and infirmities whatsoever, because Satan envieth it most, because it is a state wherein we honour God most.

I will not enter largely into the point, because I have spoken of it in other texts; but, forasmuch as concerneth this time, we must labour for that, without the which we cannot go through that which God calleth us to.

(1.) *There be many duties and dispositions that God requires which we cannot be in without assurance of salvation on good grounds*. What is that? God bids us be thankful in all things. How can I know that, unless I know God is mine and Christ is mine? Can I be thankful for that which I doubt of and think I ought to doubt of? Therefore it is such a state, without which I cannot perform other duty; and particularly the grand duty of thankfulness. And what a pitiful state is this, that a man should not be thankful for Christ, nor heaven, nor for the state of another world, that there should be such great matters, and yet they cannot thank God for them.

(2.) *Again, God enjoineth us to rejoice*. 'Rejoice, and again I say, rejoice' (Phil. 4:4). Can a man rejoice that his name is written in heaven, and not know his name is written there? The disciples were very weak now; and yet, notwithstanding all their infirmities, they loved Christ; they cast themselves upon him, and had not chosen another Saviour. Therefore 'rejoice that your names are written in heaven' (Luke 10:20), and how can a man rejoice that knoweth it not to be so? By God's writing of the law in a man's heart, he may know his name is written in heaven. Can a man always rejoice if he hath not grounds why?

(3.) Again, *God requires cheerfulness*. 'God loveth a cheerful giver' (2 Cor. 9:7), and a cheerful doer. It is the disposition that is required in everything. 'Give me thy heart' in everything thou dost (Prov. 23:26). Alas! how can I perform cheerful service to God, when I doubt whether he be my God and Father or no? Shall not I labour for a heart to yield cheerful obedience? Doth it not come deadly off? Surely it doth. We ought to comfort ourselves; and how can a man comfort himself in a condition full of uncertainties? No comforts are comfortable without this, that God is our God and our Father. Unless we know this, comforts themselves are not comfortable unto us. None of the comforts we have, the comforts of this life, are not comforts to us when the soul saith, Perhaps God feeds me to slaughter; and, perhaps, I have these mercies as my portion in this world; and how can he be comfortable when he apprehendeth not, that they issue from a spring of love? Alas! comforts themselves are uncomfortable. And therefore shall not I labour for that without which I cannot be comforted? especially it being a disposition for our good to be thankful, and cheerful, and joyful, and large-hearted.

(4.) God requires a disposition in us that we should be *full of encouragements, and strong in the Lord*; and that we should be courageous for his cause in withstanding his enemies and our enemies. How can there be courage in resisting our corruptions, Satan's temptations? How can there be courage in suffering persecution and crosses in the world, if there be not some particular interest we have in Christ and in God? It cannot be so. Unless we will deny obedience to all duty enjoined, we must have this assurance which enters into all, which is the spirit that quickeneth and enliveneth all. Therefore labour for it.

Use 2. Else *we shall take away the grounds that God enforceth good duties from in Scripture*, as he doth enforce duty from this ground, 'As elect, see ye put on bowels of compassion' (Col. 3:12). I beseech you, 'by the mercies of God, offer yourselves a sacrifice to God' (Rom. 12:1). Alas! I know not whether I shall have mercy or no. Why take away your ground and overthrow your principles? And therefore shall not we labour for that state of soul wherein we are fitted to be in that disposition, and to perform duty as God would have us? I therefore beseech you, labour for assurance of salvation.

That we may maintain it the better, see the grounds of it. It is not in our perfection, for then the poor disciples, where had they been? Alas! they had dealt unfaithfully with Christ. But the ground of firmness is on God's side, the certainty is on God's part, not ours. Tell them, 'I go to my Father, and my God; and their Father and their God.' Though we make breaches every day, yet God breaketh not, as Malachi 3:6, 'Verily, I the Lord am not changeable; and therefore you are not consumed.' We change, ebb and flow, are to and fro, up and down every day, varying in our dispositions. Though there be some root and seed of grace in us always, yet there is a change in our dispositions every day; but it holdeth on God's part. And therefore Christ nameth not any qualification in them to build comfort on, but 'my God and your God' will yet maintain the relation of a Father to you, that have not dealt as you should do; and maintaineth the relation of a God, notwithstanding your fall. So that we maintain not our assurance on any part in us, but on God's love. 'Whom he loveth, he loveth to the end' (John 13:1). Our God unchangeably loveth us, in whom there is not so much as a shadow of change. And therefore in the last of the Hebrews, it is called an 'everlasting covenant'. 'The God of peace that brought again from the dead our Lord Jesus, the great Shepherd of the sheep, through the blood of the everlasting covenant' (Heb. 13:20). By the blood of Christ there is an everlasting covenant. God will be our God to death, and in death, and for ever. For this relation being on God's part, extendeth itself from forgiveness of sins to life everlasting. It is always. The blood of Christ is the blood of an everlasting covenant. 'I will marry thee to me for ever' (Hos. 2:19). It holdeth sure on God's part.

Let us labour to maintain this assurance of salvation from God's love.

Use 3. But for our comfort, *we must do our parts too, though it begin with God*. It beginneth on God's part. He loveth us first, and embraceth us first; and we must love again, and embrace again. We must desire of God grace to answer relation. Therefore I will prescribe some rules, how we may say, God is our God, with comfort. That we may have the comfort of it, by making good our interest in him, to make it good that we are sons, as well as to call him Father; that we are his people, as well as to call him our God; his spouse, as well as call him our husband. And because this cometh from God, join this with all our endeavours: Lord, thou must begin; I desire to show myself as a spouse to thee; but thou must discover thyself to me. I desire to love thee, but discover thy love first; all I can do is but reflection. Thou must shine on me first. So desire God to reveal himself more and more in Christ Jesus; and then we cannot but carry ourselves to him as we should do in our relation.

This day we must perform the relation on our sides. There be two words that go to this heavenly bargain. The covenant consisteth of two parts. Now, desire God, by his grace, to enable us to do our part, for he doth both. And desire him, according to his promise, to teach us to love him, and 'to write his law in our hearts' (Jer. 31:33), to do what is good; and circumcise our hearts, and give his Holy Spirit. We ask no more than he hath promised, and so go boldly to him. Lord, thou hast made a covenant with us; we cannot keep it without thee. Thou hast not only promised grace and gifts, but the grace to perform the covenant on our parts must come from thee. And this God will do. Therefore in the use of means, attend upon him; and looking to him, we shall have grace to do our parts, and then maintain this assurance, without which we cannot live as Christians should live.

That we may further maintain this relation, that God is our God, let us labour to get into Christ, for it is in him that God is our Father; and to grow up in Christ, to grow more and more, to grow up in faith and in all grace.

A gracious Christian never wanteth arguments of assurance of salvation. It is the dead-hearted Christian, the careless Christian. Therefore labour, as to be in Christ, so to grow up in the knowledge of Christ.

And so to know God in Christ, labour to see the face of God in Christ; for in him are all the beams of his love. As the beams of the sun in a glass are gathered, so the beams of all God's love meet in Christ. So lovely is God in Christ, whatsoever we have in Christ it is from God in Christ. And whatsoever we have from God, it is through Christ; therefore grow in the knowledge of Christ, in faith in Christ. To this end are the sacraments, that we might grow up in him, and be fed into Christ. And then we may make right use of it, as the ordinance that God hath sanctified for this end. And as God doth take us out and set a stamp upon us, so labour to make choice of God more and more, and choice of God in Christ; for there be the two objects of our faith and love. Choose God for our God, and esteem him above all, and renounce all other, and resign ourselves wholly to him; for all is ours when God is ours. He setteth us apart from other men – taking us out – and appropriateth us to himself, chooseth us for his jewels. I beseech you, labour daily to choose God to be your God. If we say, we are God's, let us make choice of him at the same time, and appropriate him with our choice. He is mine in particular. There is renunciation of all others. I have served other gods heretofore; the world, and the flesh, and the favour of man have been my god, but they shall be my god no more. If we choose him not, and appropriate him as ours, and renounce all other, and give ourselves to him, we cannot say he is 'our God'. This we should practise every day. In the solicitation of sin, or despair for sin, make use of this choice, and appropriation, and resignation. If we be tempted to any sin, Why, I am not mine own, I am God's. I have chosen him to be my God; I have appropriated myself to him; I have renounced all other; I have offered myself to him; therefore what have I to do with sin, with this temptation? I have taken the sacrament on it, that God is mine, and Christ is mine, with all his benefits. Therefore if there be any solicitation to sin, make this use of it; and so we shall grow in assurance of our interest in God, when we can make use of it on all occasions.

If when we be moved to any sin, by Satan, or our own flesh, which is a devil within us, This is contrary to my covenant, this is contrary to the renewing of the covenant, so often renewed in the sacrament, and therefore I will not commit it. It is contrary to the state I am advanced to, and contrary to my relation. God is my Father and my God, and therefore I must be his; and what have I to do with sin? What hath pride to do with a heart bequeathed to God? What hath lust and filthiness? What hath injustice, or anything else that is sinful, to do in a heart that hath dedicated and consecrated itself to God, who hath given up himself and all he can do, and to whom we have given up all we have? and shall we give our strength to sin and Satan, his enemies?

Thus we should grow in assurance, exercising the increase and knowledge of our interest. I beseech you, therefore, let us use these and the like things to make God our God. And if any temptation to sin be joined, as Satan cannot but solicit to sin, so he laboureth when we have sinned to tempt to despair for sin; for they be the two ways by which Satan prevails. Now, fetch comfort against both from hence, 'God is my God and my Father', and Christ teacheth them to call him so; and therefore, notwithstanding sin, I may go to God and call him Father. The disciples, though their sin was great, yet on their humility they were to acknowledge God to be their Father and their God. And therefore answer Satan: I ought not to abuse, and break off, and deny my interest in God as my Father and my God for any sin, because the disciples did not so; and Christ hath taught how to make use of God, and to acknowledge him for my comfort. We cannot have a better guide than God; and therefore never think of God but as 'our God and our Father', and labour to answer all Satan's temptations in that kind from hence.

Use 4. Again, This assurance, that God is our God in Christ, and our Father, *is wrought by the sealing of the Spirit*, and sanctifying of us; therefore take heed we grieve not the Spirit of God. God's Spirit moveth our hearts oftentimes in hearing the word, or reading, or praying; when we have any good motions, or when we entertain them; and therefore do not grieve the Spirit of God, whose office is 'to seal us to the day of redemption', to assure us God is our God and our Father in Christ. Grieve him not, lest he grieve us, by racking and tormenting our consciences. That is the way to maintain our interest. Take heed of crossing the Spirit, especially by any sin against conscience. Conscience is God's deputy. Grieve not the Spirit. Grieve not conscience, for conscience is God's deputative. It is a little god within us. And therefore, if we will not alienate God from us, to whom we have given ourselves if we be true believers, do nothing against his deputy and agent, the Spirit that sanctifieth and sealeth us to the day of redemption.

This is the way to maintain assurance, that God is our God. For men may be led with a spirit of presumption, and say, God is my God. But if conscience telleth them, they live in sin against conscience and the motions of the Spirit, and suppress them, and kill them, as births that they would not have grow in their hearts; then they cannot say God is my God, but conscience telleth them they lie. And therefore, I beseech you, labour for an holy life. That faith that maketh this claim, that God is my Father and my God, is a purifying faith (1 John 3:3). It is a faith quickening the soul, a faith purifying, a faith cleansing. Faith is wonderfully operative, especially having these promises. What promises? 'I will be your God and your Father.' 'Having such promises, let us cleanse ourselves from all filthiness of flesh and spirit, and grow up in all holiness in the fear of the Lord.' And therefore labour for that faith that layeth hold upon this privilege, God is our Father and our God. Make it good by this, that it be a purifying faith, an operative faith, that worketh by love, that showeth itself in our conversation. The more we labour and grow this way, the more we grow in assurance of salvation.

Beloved, favour cannot be maintained with great persons without much industry, and respect, and observance of distance. A man that will maintain the favour of great persons must be well read in their dispositions, must know how to please them, and yield them all observance and respect. And shall we think then to preserve respect with God without much industry and holiness? It cannot be. 'And therefore give all diligence', not a little, 'to make your calling and election sure' (2 Pet. 1:10). It requireth all diligence, it is worth your pains. We live on this, that he is our God, and will be our God to death and in death, for ever and ever. That God is our God to everlasting, that he is of an equal extent with the soul, he liveth to fill it and make it happy, our souls being of an eternal subsistence. Therefore it standeth us upon 'to give all diligence to make our calling and election sure', else it will not be maintained. Why do not Christians enjoy the comforts of this, that God is their God in Christ, more than they do? The reason is, they be negligent to maintain intercourse between God and them. We must know our distances, there must be reverent carriage to God (Psa. 2:11). A loose Christian can never enjoy the comforts of God. He is so great, and we so mean, we ought to reverence him, we ought to 'love him with fear, and rejoice with trembling' (Psa. 2:11). Humble thyself to walk with thy God. Where there is a great deal of humility, it maintaineth friendship. We cannot walk with God as a friend, as Abraham is said to be God's friend. We must acknowledge ourselves to be 'dust and ashes', know him in his greatness, and ourselves in our meanness, if he will maintain this to our hearts, that God is our God. If we be careful to maintain this, surely he that delighteth himself in the prosperity of his servants will delight to make himself more and more known to us, that we may be assured of our salvation.

All that hear me are such as have not yet made choice of God to be their God, or have made choice. Let me speak a word to both; for there be many that yet have their choice to make, that have other lords and other gods to rule over them. Let them consider what a fearful state it is not to be able to say, in regard of life everlasting, 'God is my God and my Father.' They can say they be God's creatures; but what a fearful condition is it not to be able to say, God is my Father. Will not these know whom he is not a God to in favour, he will be a God to in vengeance? He must be a friend or enemy.

There is no third in God. God and the devil divide all mankind. They share all. If thou be not God's, and canst not say so on good titles, thou art the devil's. Yet God is daily pulling men out of the kingdom of the devil, by opening their eyes to see their miserable condition; yet all go under these two grand titles, God's, and the devil's. If thou canst not say, God is thy God, then the devil is thy god; and what a fearful condition is it to be under the god of the world by a worldly, carnal disposition! And perhaps thou mayest die so, if thou be not careful to get out of it. If God be not our God, he is our enemy; and then creatures, angels, devils are against us, conscience against us, word against us. If he be for us, who is against us? If he be against us, who is for us? A terrible condition, and therefore get out of it, I beseech you.

But how shall I do? Is there mercy for such a wretch? Yea, he offereth himself to be thy God if thou wilt come in. Wherefore serveth our ministry, the word of grace, but to preach life to all repentant sinners. 'He that confesseth and forsaketh his sins shall have mercy.' And therefore God hath ordained ambassadors of peace to proclaim if you will come in. And he entreateth you to come in, and he chargeth and commandeth you. You be rebels, not only against him, but enemies to your own souls if you do not. And therefore I beseech you, if you be not yet come in. Add this more, you be sacrilegious persons if you be not Christians in earnest. Have not you given yourselves to God in baptism? And have not you in your lives given yourselves to lusts which you renounced at your baptism? Now you have alienated yourselves from God, to whom you were dedicated. Did not you engage yourselves to God in your baptism? And is not he willing to receive you? He thought of you when you could not think of yourselves. And therefore, as it bindeth you over to greater punishment if you will not come in, but continue sacrilegious persons from God to whom you have dedicated yourselves, so God preventeth[1] you with mercy.

He encourageth by the seal of election in baptism to make it good by faith, without which it will do no good, being but a seal to a blank. Therefore how many encouragements have you to come in? Take God's gracious offer. He giveth you time. Make your peace. It is nothing but wilful rebellion to stand out against God.

For they that have given themselves to God, and now renewed their interest in him by the sacraments, let them conceive what a word of comfort they have in this, *that Christ is theirs and God is theirs*. What an ocean of comforts is it when all things leave you, as all things will; yet we have God, that will be a God for evermore. At the time of death, what comfort will it be to say, God is mine, Christ is mine. Life is mine no longer; world is mine no longer; friends forsake me, but I am interested in God, and have made covenant with God, who is a God for ever. The covenant I have made is an

[1] That is, = 'God has come before with mercy, *e.g.*, baptism', *etc.*—G.

'everlasting covenant'. It is of that largeness, the comfort
is, that the angels themselves admire it,[1] the devils
envy it, and it is a matter of glory and praise in heaven
for ever. Therefore make much of such a privilege,
that is the envy of devils, the admiration of angels,
that is the joy of a Christian's heart here, and matter
of glorifying God for ever, world without end. That
God in Christ is become his God here and for ever, it
is a ravishing consideration. It is larger than our hearts.
Here be comforts larger than the capacity of our hearts.
Cor vestrum soli Deo patere debet: our hearts ought all
to lie open to divine things, for they have more in them
than the heart can contain. If we will shut them, shut
them to worldly things. Oh the comfort of a Christian
that hath made his state sure: let him glory in the Lord.

There be three degrees of glory in all. Let him glory
under hope of glory, glory in afflictions, and glory in
God; that is, we glory in God to be our God. That in
the sharing and dividing of all things God hath given
himself to us; and what an offer is this, that when God
divideth this world to the children of men, you shall
have this and that, but you shall not have me. But to
his children he hath given himself, and he hath nothing
better to give, and indeed there is nothing else needs.
For there is more in it than we can speak. But that when
God divideth all things he should give such a share as
himself, is not this a glory, that a poor creature should

---

[1] That is, 'wonder'.—G.

have God to be his, and all he hath to be his, to make use of it in life and in death? It is worth all the world; it is worth our endeavours 'to make our calling and election sure', when we may have this comfort from it (2 Pet. 1:10).

―――――――――――

BANNER *of* **TRUTH**

THE Banner of Truth Trust originated in 1957 in London. The founders believed that much of the best literature of historic Christianity had been allowed to fall into oblivion and that, under God, its recovery could well lead not only to a strengthening of the church, but to true revival.

Inter-denominational in vision, this publishing work is now international, and our lists include a number of contemporary authors along with classics from the past. The translation of these books into many languages is encouraged.

A monthly magazine, *The Banner of Truth*, is also published. More information about this and all our publications can be found on our website or supplied by either of the offices below.

Head Office:
3 Murrayfield Road
Edinburgh
EH12 6EL
United Kingdom
Email: info@banneroftruth.co.uk

North America Office:
PO Box 621
Carlisle, PA 17013
United States of America
Email: info@banneroftruth.org